FARADAY'S

CHEMICAL HISTORY

OF A CANDLE

FARADAY'S

CHEMICAL HISTORY

OF A CANDLE

Michael Faraday

Chicago Review Press

Library of Congress Cataloging—in—Publication Data

Faraday, Michael, 1791–1867.
 (Course of six lectures on the chemical history of a candle)
 Faraday's chemical history of a candle: six illustrated lectures with
notes and experiments / by Michael Faraday. — 1st ed.
 p. cm.
 Originally published as: A course of six lectures on the chemical
history of the candle. 1861.
 Includes index.
 Summary: Presents a newly illustrated edition of Faraday's six classic
lectures that provide an introduction to the principles of combustion.
Includes twenty-two experiments that demonstrate the argument of the
lectures.
 ISBN 1-556-52035-2 (pbk.) : $9.95
 1. Chemistry—Juvenile literature. 2. Candles—Juvenile literature.
[1. Chemistry. 2. Candles. 3. Experiments.]
I. Title. II. Title: Chemical history of a candle.
QD39.F2 1988
540-dc19 88-19006

Printed in the United States of America
First Edition

Published by Chicago Review Press, Incorporated
814 N. Franklin, Chicago, Illinois 60610

To Les Siemens, with thanks

CONTENTS

Experiments 83

List of Illustrations

Introduction

How these lectures
came to be written

Young Michael Faraday

In 1812 Michael Faraday was twenty-one years old. His 7-year apprenticeship to the bookbinder, Mr. G. Riebau, had just terminated. It seemed as if his study of science was ending as well. Michael's family was poor, and he had been apprenticed when he was fourteen. He had enjoyed working in Riebau's shop, where he was allowed to spend almost as much time reading books as he did binding them. He became interested in electricity while binding a volume of the *Encyclopedia Britannica* in which the subject was discussed. Other scientific topics interested him as well, and he even tried to set up a small after-hours laboratory behind the shop. He attended scientific lectures whenever he could and took voluminous notes.

In 1812 Michael feared that he would have to give up all these pleasant pastimes and set about the dreary business of earning a hard living. He knew that with little or no time to devote to science and with no proper laboratory—to say nothing of teachers—he didn't have much chance of becoming more than a dabbler in science.

Discouraged, he wrote to a friend " . . . since then [the end of his apprenticeship] I have had far less time and liberty than before. . . [I] am now working at my old trade. . . . I must resign philosophy [science] to those who are more fortunate in the possesssion of time and means."

In desperation Faraday sent letters off to anyone he could think of who might help him find work, however menial, that would allow him to be in a scientific laboratory. He wrote pleadingly to Sir Joseph Banks, then president of the Royal Society, and did not even receive a reply.

His first break came late in October when Sir Humphrey Davy, experimenting a little recklessly, injured his eyes and was unable to read or write for several days. On the recommendation of a friend, Davy took young Faraday on as a temporary secretary. The acquaintance (and the job) was brief, but evidently Michael made a good impression. The following spring, when William Payne, the "fag and scrub" at the Royal Institution, was caught brawling and got himself summarily dismissed from his job, Faraday was offered the position. He was offered free lodging in two rooms on an upper floor of the Royal Institution Building on Albemarle Street, plus money for candles and a guinea a week wages.

Michael had no illusions that the job would involve anything but a lot of menial chores and hard work, but he eagerly accepted when Davy agreed to permit him to work in the laboratory on his own time. From that time forth Michael Faraday's life became inextricably linked with the fate of the Royal Institution of Great Britain.

The Royal Institution

The name "Royal Institution of Great Britain" is likely to conjure up the image of a staid, "established-since-the-reign-of-Queen-Elizabeth" entity. This was far from true. The Institution had been founded in London only about twelve years earlier by a colorful but not very popular refugee from the American colonies, Benjamin Thompson.

Benjamin Thompson (George III later made him Count

Rumford) was born in Woburn, Massachusetts. A Loyalist during the Revolution, he served as a British spy after the outbreak of the war for independence and was forced to flee to London in 1776. Later in the war he commanded a British regiment in New York. Returning to the Old World, he dedicated himself to the study of physics, especially of heat, and worked a great deal on practical inventions such as improved fireplaces and chimneys. He also invented the double boiler, a kitchen stove and a percolating coffee pot.

He was not known for his modesty and his chief aim in founding the Royal Institution seemed to be to publicize his own inventions, which he planned to display there. His egotism got in the way whenever he tried to raise money for his pet project, but finally, by around 1800, the Institution had acquired a building and a few professors. Contented with his handiwork, the inventor left England never to return. He died in France in 1814.

Faraday at the Royal Institution
The Institution spent the first few decades of its existence foundering on the brink of total bankruptcy, just scraping through one year at a time. In 1813, when Faraday was on leave in France with Sir Humphrey Davy (Faraday acting as a sort of combination scientific assistant and valet), they heard that the Institution was going through one of its periodic financial crises. Hastily, Michael wrote to a friend in London, begging him to rush over to Albemarle Street to claim some personal belongings (mainly books) that Faraday had left at the Institution, so that they would not be sold up when the Institution went under.

He later received a reply from his friend assuring him that indeed things *had* looked pretty black but a last-minute sub-scription had been gathered, and the Royal Institution had once again escaped disaster. At least, it should last until Michael could get back to England and claim his books for himself.

Before long, Michael Faraday became as important to the

Royal Institution as it had been to him. He was grateful for the chance it had given him to fulfill his dream of becoming a scientist. In return, Faraday almost single-handedly made possible the survival of the Royal Institution. He had a tremendous natural talent for devising experiments, and he built on this talent by hard and painstaking study. Over the years he completed many scientific commissions which earned money for the Institution; these projects ranged from testing the various grades of oatmeal used aboard the ships of the British Navy to making intricate studies of the production of high-quality steel and optical glass.

The Lectures

An important feature of the Royal Institution as envisaged by its founder was the dissemination of knowledge of "useful mechanical inventions and improvements and . . . the application of science to the common purposes of life." The problem was to present lectures which were entertaining— instruction that people would be willing to pay good money to hear—no easier then than it is today. These lectures were one of the major sources of revenue for the Institution.

Faraday made his first appearance on the lecture stage as an experimental assistant to William Brande. As Brande talked, Faraday smoothly worked the demonstrations for him. Brande was a capable if uninspired lecturer, and his assistant probably formed a few ideas of his own about what made a good lecture. Before long Faraday had the opportunity to give some lectures himself, and, after he conquered the stage fright that forced him to write out his first lectures word for word, he became a proficient, even dazzling, lecturer, working his own experiments as he talked—the way a magician works his illusions.

In the course of the next forty and more years, Faraday gave hundreds of lectures in the theater of the Royal Institution. Two lecture series attracted large general audiences. The first, started in 1825, were the Friday Evening Discourses

for members of the Institution and their guests and friends. (Among the topics were electricity, the silvering of mirrors, and lighthouse illumination.) The second series were the Juvenile or "Christmas" lectures, so-called because they were given for young people during their Christmas holidays. Faraday particularly liked speaking to a younger audience and his lectures were enthusiastically received, especially "On the Various Forces of Matter" and "The Chemical History of a Candle." These were often repeated by popular demand, and in the 1850's Faraday gave permission to have a stenographer take them down, as delivered.

At the end of his career in 1861, when Michael Faraday made the decision to resign from the Royal Institution he spoke poignantly of the particular enjoyment he took in giving these lectures.

Gentlemen: [he wrote]
. . . I entered the Royal Institution in March 1813, nearly forty-nine years ago; and . . . have been with you ever since . . . My life has been a happy one and all that I could have desired. During its progress I have tried to make a fitting return for it to the Royal Institution and through it to Science.
. . . I now ask you to accept my resignation of the Juvenile lectures. Being unwilling to give up, what has always been so kindly received and so pleasant to myself, I have tried the faculties essential for their delivery, and I know I ought to retreat; . . . I desire therefore to lay down this duty; and I may truly say, that such has been the pleasure of the occupation to me, that my regret must be greater than yours need or can be."

Michael Faraday died in 1867.

The Scientific Discoveries of Michael Faraday

1820 discovered two unknown chlorides of carbon

1821 discovered electromagnetic rotation—set up an experiment in which a wire carrying an electric current rotated in the field of a horseshoe magnet.

1823 liquified chlorine

1825 isolated benzene

1831 demonstrated the principle of electromagnetic induction—the production of electric current by a change in magnetic intensity

1844 discovered the rotation of the plane of polarization of light in a magnetic field.

3786
-1223

43775
1380

1777

43775
+ 1485
45260

- 105
45155

45155
- 3000
42155

21.0775
42.1550
63.2325
× (5)

45155

4+1=8

8+1+

15+4

Banks 21'.03

Brenda

43775
+ 0
1485

45.360
- 105.
45195

4
45195
- 12700
32495

4656 exemptus

32495
x 2
20250
12245

Lecture I

A Candle—The Flame—Its Sources—Mobility & Brightness

I propose to bring before you, in the course of these lectures, the Chemical History of a Candle. There is not a law under which any part of this universe is governed which does not come into play and is touched upon in these phenomena. There is no better, there is no more open door by which you can enter into the study of natural philosophy than by considering the physical phenomena of a candle.

A Candle

Here are a couple of candles commonly called dips. They are made of lengths of cotton cut off, hung up by a loop, dipped into melted tallow, taken out again and cooled, then redipped, until there is an accumulation of tallow round the cotton....The candle I have in my hand is a stearin candle, made of stearin from tallow. Then here is a sperm candle, which comes from the purified oil of the spermaceti whale. Here, also, are yellow bee's-wax, from which candles are made. Here, too, is that curious substance called paraffine, and some paraffine candles, made of paraffine obtained from the bogs of Ireland.

By natural philosophy, Faraday meant the study of the natural world and the causes and effects operating in it. He always preferred to call himself a natural philosopher rather than a physicist or chemist.

Stearin is the solid, as opposed to the oily, part of a fatty substance.

Paraffine is a fatty material obtained from petroleum.

1

And how are these candles made? I have told you about dips, and I will show you how molds are made. Let us imagine any of these candles to be made of materials which can be cast. "Cast!" you say. "Why, a candle is a thing that melts, and surely if you can melt it you can cast it." Not so. It is wonderful, in the progress of manufacture, and in the consideration of the means best fitted to produce the required result, how things turn up which one would not expect beforehand. Candles can not always be cast. A wax candle can never be cast. It is made by a particular process which I can illustrate in a minute or two, but I must not spend much time on it. Wax is a thing which, burning so well, and melting so easily in a candle, can not be cast. However, let us take a material that can be cast. Here is a frame, with a number of molds fastened to it. The first thing to be done is to put a wick through them. Here is one—a plaited wick, which does not require snuffing—supported by a little wire. It goes to the bottom, where it is pegged in; the little peg holding the cotton tight, and stopping the aperture so that nothing fluid shall run out. At the upper part there is a little bar placed across, which stretches the cotton and holds it in the mold. The tallow is then melted, and the molds are filled. After a certain time, when the molds are cool, the excess of tallow is poured off at one corner, and then cleaned off altogether, and the end of the wick cut away. The candles alone then remain in the mold, and you have only to upset them, as I am doing, when out they tumble, for the candles are made in the form of cones, being narrower at the top than at the bottom; so that, what with their form and their own shrinking, they only need a little shaking and out they fall. In the same way are made these candles of stearin and of paraffine. It is a curious thing to see how wax candles are made. A lot of cottons are hung upon frame, as you see here, and covered with metal tags at the ends to keep the wax from covering the cotton in those places. These are carried to a heater, where the wax is melted. As you see, the frames can

turn round; and, as they turn, a man takes a vessel of wax and pours it first down one, and then the next, and the next, and so on. When he has gone once round, if it is sufficiently cool, he gives the first a second coat, and so on until they are all of the required thickness. When they have been thus clothed, or fed, or made up to that thickness, they are taken off and placed elsewhere. I have here, by the kindness of Mr. Field, several specimens of these candles. Here is one only half finished. They are then taken down and well rolled upon a fine stone slab, and the conical top is moulded by properly shaped tubes, and the bottoms cut off and trimmed. This is done so beautifully that they can make candles in this way weighing exactly four or six to the pound, or any number they please.

We must not, however, take up more time about the mere manufacture, but go a little farther into the matter. I have not yet referred you to luxuries in candles (for there is such a thing as luxury in candles). See how beautifully these are colored; you see here mauve, magenta, and all the chemical colors recently introduced, applied to candles. You observe, also, different forms employed. Here is a fluted pillar most beautifully shaped; and I have also here some candles sent me by Mr. Pearsall, which are ornamented with designs upon them, so that, as they burn, they have, as it were, a glowing sun above, and a bouquet of flowers beneath. All, however, that is fine and beautiful is not useful. These fluted candles, pretty as they are, are bad candles; they are bad because of their external shape. Nevertheless, I show you these specimens, sent to me from kind friends on all sides, that you may see what is done and what may be done in this or that direction; although, as I have said, when we come to these refinements, we are obliged to sacrifice a little in utility.

Sources of the Flame

Now as to the light of the candle. We will light one or two, and set them at work in the performance of their proper functions. You observe a candle is a very different thing from a lamp. With a lamp you take a little oil, fill your vessel, put in a little moss or some cotton prepared by artificial means,

and then light the top of the wick. When the flame goes down the cotton to the oil, it gets extinguished, but it goes on burning in the part above. Now I have no doubt you will ask how it is that the oil which will not burn of itself gets up to the top of the cotton, where it will burn. We shall presently examine that; but there is a much more wonderful thing about the burning of a candle than this. You have here a solid substance with no vessel to contain it, and how is it that this solid substance can get up to the place where the flame is? How is it that this solid gets there, it not being a fluid? Or, when it is made a fluid, then how is it that it keeps together? This is a wonderful thing about a candle.

We have here a good deal of wind, which will help us in some of our illustrations, but tease us in others; for the sake, therefore, of a little regularity, and to simplify the matter, I shall make a quiet flame, for who can study a subject when there are difficulties in the way not belonging to it? Here is a clever invention of some costermonger or street-stander in the market-place for the shading of their candles on Saturday night, when they are selling their greens, or potatoes, or fish. I have very often admired it. They put a lamp-glass round the candle, supported on a kind of gallery, which clasps it, and it can be slipped up and down as required. By the use of this lamp-glass, employed in the same way, you have a steady flame, which you can look at, and carefully examine, as I hope you will do, at home.

You see then, in the first instance, that a beautiful cup is formed. As the air comes to the candle, it moves upward by the force of the current which the heat of the candle produces, and it so cools all the sides of the wax, tallow, or fuel as to keep the edge much cooler than the part within; the part within melts by the flame that runs down the wick as far as it can go before it is extinguished, but the part on the outside does not melt. If I made a current in one direction, my cup would be lop-sided, and the fluid would consequently run over; for the same force of gravity which

LAMP GLASS
In this device for protecting the candle from drafts, a chimney is supported around the candle by means of a gallery which allows it to be slipped up or down as required.

holds worlds together holds this fluid in a horizontal position, and if the cup be not horizontal, of course the fluid will run away in guttering. You see, therefore, that the cup is formed by this beautifully regular ascending current of air playing upon all sides, which keeps the exterior of the candle cool. No fuel would serve for a candle which has not the property of giving this cup, except such fuel as the Irish bog-wood, where the material itself is like a sponge and holds its own fuel. You see now why these beautiful candles that I have shown you, which are irregular, intermittent in their shape, and can not, therefore, have that nicely-formed edge to the cup which is the great beauty in a candle. I hope you will see that the perfection of a process—that is, its utility—is the better point of beauty about it. It is not the best looking thing, but the best acting thing, which is the most advantageous to us. This good-looking candle is a bad-burning one. There will be a guttering round about it because of the irregularity of the stream of air and the badness of the cup which is formed thereby. You may see some pretty examples (and I trust you will notice these instances) of the action of the ascending current when you have a little gutter run down the side of a candle, making it thicker there than it is elsewhere. As the candle goes on burning, that keeps its place and forms a little pillar sticking up by the side, because as it rises higher about the rest of the wax or fuel, the air gets better round it, and it is more cooled and better able to resist the action of the heat at a little distance. Now the greatest mistakes and faults with regard to candles, as in many other things, often bring with them instruction which we should not receive if they had not occurred. We come here to be philosophers, and I hope you will always remember that whenever a result happens, especially if it be new, you should say, "What is the cause? Why does it occur?" and you will, in the course of time, find out the reason.

Then there is another point about these candles which will answer a question—that is, as to the way in which this fluid

Irish bogwood is the wood of trees preserved in the peat bogs of Ireland.

Decorated candles are not necessarily the most functional ones. The irregular air currents rising around the stem of this candle will cause poor cup formation and a guttering flame.

gets out of the cup, up the wick, and into the place of combustion. You know that the flames on these burning wicks in candles made of bees'-wax, stearin, or spermaceti, do not run down to the wax or other matter, and melt it all away, but keep to their own right place. They are fenced off from the fluid below, and do not encroach on the cup at the sides. I can not imagine a more beautiful example than the condition of adjustment under which a candle makes one part subserve to the other to the very end of its action. A combustible thing like that, burning away gradually, never being intruded upon by the flame, is a very beautiful sight, especially when you come to learn what a vigorous thing flame is—what power it has of destroying the wax itself when it gets hold of it, and of disturbing its proper form if it come only too near.

But how does the flame get hold of the fuel? There is a beautiful point about that—*capillary attraction.* "Capillary attraction!" you say—"the attraction of hairs." Well, never mind the name; it was given in old times before we had a good understanding of what the real power was. It is by what is called capillary attraction that the fuel is conveyed to the part where combustion goes on, and is deposited there, not in a careless way, but very beautifully in the very midst of the center of action, which takes place around it. Now I am going to give you one or two instances of capillary attraction. It is that kind of action or attraction which makes two things that do not dissolve in each other still hold together. When you wash your hands, you wet them thoroughly; you take a little soap to make the adhesion better, and you find your hands remain wet. This is by that kind of attraction of which I am about to speak. And, what is more, if your hands are not soiled (as they almost always are by the usages of life), if you put your finger into a little warm water, the water will creep a little way up the finger, though you may not stop to examine it. I have here a substance which is rather porous—a column of salt—and I will pour into the plate at the bottom, not

water, as it appears, but a saturated solution of salt which can not absorb more, so that the action which you see will not be due to its dissolving any thing. We may consider the plate to be the candle, and the salt the wick, and this solution the melted tallow. (I have colored the fluid, that you may see the action better.) You observe that, now I pour in the fluid, it rises and gradually creeps up the salt higher and higher; and provided the column does not tumble over, it will go to the top. If this blue solution were combustible, and we were to place a wick at the top of the salt, it would burn as it entered into the wick. It is a most curious thing to see this kind of action taking place, and to observe how singular some of the circumstances are about it. When you wash your hands, you take a towel to wipe off the water; and it is by that kind of wetting, or that kind of attraction which makes the towel become wet with water, that the wick is made wet with the tallow. I have known some careless boys and girls (indeed, I have known it happen to careful people as well) who, having washed their hands and wiped them with a towel, have thrown the towel over the side of the basin, and before long it has drawn all the water out of the basin and conveyed it to the floor, because it happened to be thrown over the side in such a way as to serve the purpose of a siphon. That you may the better see the way in which the substances act one upon another, I have here a vessel made of wire gauze filled with water, and you may compare it in its action to the cotton in one respect, or to a piece of calico on the other. In fact, wicks are sometimes made of a kind of wire gauze. You will observe that this vessel is a porous thing; for if I pour a little water on to the top, it will run out at the bottom. You would be puzzled for a good while if I asked you what the state of this vessel is, what is inside it, and why it is there? The vessel is full of water, and yet you see the water goes in and runs out as if it were empty. In order to prove this to you I have only to empty it. The reason is this: the wire, being once wetted, remains wet; the meshes

Capillary attraction causes the saturated salt solution to be absorbed in the column of salt even though the solution cannot dissolve any more salt.

By wire gauze Faraday meant what we would call a metal sieve or strainer.

7

are so small that the fluid is attracted so strongly from the one side to the other as to remain in the vessel, although it is porous. In like manner, the particles of melted tallow ascend the cotton and get to the top; other particles then follow by their mutual attraction for each other, and as they reach the flame they are gradually burned.

Here is another application of the same principle. You see this bit of cane. If I place this piece of cane on a plate containing some camphene (which is very much like paraffine in its general character), exactly in the same manner as the blue fluid rose through the salt will this fluid rise through the piece of cane. There being no pores at the side, the fluid can not go in that direction, but must pass through its length. Already the fluid is at the top of the cane; now I can light it and make it serve as a candle. The fluid has risen by the capillary attraction of the piece of cane, just as it does through the cotton in the candle.

Now the only reason why the candle does not burn all down the side of the wick is that the melted tallow extinguishes the flame. You know that a candle, if turned upside down, so as to allow the fuel to run upon the wick, will be put out. The reason is, that the flame has not had time to make the fuel hot enough to burn, as it does above, where it is carried in small quantities into the wick, and has all the effect of the heat exercised upon it.

There is another condition which you must learn as regards the candle, without which you would not be able fully to understand the philosophy of it, and that is the vaporous condition of the fuel. In order that you may understand that let me show you a very pretty but very commonplace experiment. If you blow a candle out cleverly, you will see the vapor rise from it. You have, I know, often smelt the vapor of a blown-out candle, and a very bad smell it is; but if you blow it out cleverly you will be able to see pretty well the vapor into which this solid matter is transformed. I will blow out one of these candles in such a way as not to disturb the

Camphene is a rectified oil of turpentine, used for lamp fuel.

The hot vapor from a just-extinguished candle can be used to light the candle remotely. The flame travels along the vapor trail to the candle-wick where the vapor originates.

EXPERIMENT 1, p. 85

8

air around it by the continuing action of my breath; and now, if I hold a lighted taper two or three inches from the wick, you will observe a train of fire going through the air till it reaches the candle. I am obliged to be quick and ready, because if I allow the vapor time to cool, it becomes condensed into a liquid or solid, or the stream of combustible matter gets disturbed.

Structure of the Flame

Let us look a little at the form of the flame as you see it under the glass shade. It is steady and equal, and its general form is that which is represented in the diagram, varying with atmospheric disturbances, and also varying according to the size of the candle. It is a bright oblong, brighter at the top than toward the bottom, with the wick in the middle, and besides the wick in the middle, certain darker parts towards the bottom, where the ignition is not so perfect as in the part above. There is a current formed, which draws the flame out; for the flame which you see is really drawn out by the current, and drawn upward to a great height . . .

EXPERIMENT 2, p. 87

by that prolongation of the current in the diagram. You may see this by taking a lighted candle, and putting it in the sun so as to get its shadow thrown on a piece of paper. How remarkable it is that that thing which is light enough to produce shadows of other objects can be made to throw its own shadow on a piece of white paper or card, so that you can actually see streaming round the flame something which is not part of the flame, but is ascending and drawing the flame upward. Now I am going to imitate the sunlight by applying the voltaic battery to the electric lamp. You now see our sun and its great luminosity; and by placing a candle between it and the screen, we get the shadow of the flame. You observe the shadow of the candle and of the wick; then there is a darkish part, as represented in the diagram, and then a part which is more distinct. Curiously enough, however, what we see in the shadow as the darkest part of the flame is, in reality, the brightest part; and here you see streaming upward the ascending current of hot air which draws out the flame, supplies it with air, and cools the sides of the cup of melted fuel.

I can give you here a little farther illustration, for the purpose of showing you how flame goes up or down according to the current. I have here a flame—it is not a candle flame—but you can, no doubt, by this time generalize enough to be able to compare one thing with another: what I am about to do is to change the ascending current that takes the flame upward into a descending current. This I can easily do by the little apparatus you see before me. The flame, as I have said, is not a candle flame, but it is produced by alcohol, so that it shall not smoke too much. I will also color the flame with another substance, so that you may trace its course; for, with the spirit alone, you could hardly see well enough to have the opportunity of tracing its direction. By lighting this spirit of wine we have then a flame produced, and you observe that when held in the air it naturally goes upward. You understand now, easily enough, why flames go

The alcohol contained chloride of copper, which produced a green flame.

10

up under ordinary circumstances: it is because of the draft of air by which the combustion is formed. But now, by blowing the flame down, you see I am enabled to make it go downward into this little chimney, the direction of the current being changed. Before we have concluded this course of lectures we shall show you a lamp in which the flame goes up and the smoke goes down, or the flame goes down and the smoke goes up. You see, then, that we have the power in this way of varying the flame in different directions.

The Mobility and Brightness of the Flame

There are now some other points that I must bring before you. Many of the flames you see here vary very much in their shape by the currents of air blowing around them in different directions; but we can, if we like, make flames so that they will look like fixtures, and we can photograph them—indeed, we have to photograph them—so that they become fixed to us, if we wish to find out every thing concerning them. That, however, is not the only thing I wish to mention. If I take a flame sufficiently large, it does not keep that homogeneous, that uniform condition of shape, but it breaks out with a power of life which is quite wonderful. I am about to use another kind of fuel, but one which is truly and fairly a representative of the wax or tallow of a candle. I have here a large ball of cotton, which will serve as a wick. And, now that I have immersed it in spirit and applied a light to it, in what way does it differ from an ordinary candle? Why, it differs very much in one respect, that we have a vivacity and power about it, a beauty and a life entirely different from the light presented by a candle. You see those fine tongues of flame rising up. You have the same general disposition of the mass of the flame from below upward, but, in addition to that, you have this remarkable breaking out into tongues which you do not perceive in the case of a candle. Now, why is this? I must explain it to you, because, when you understand that perfectly, you will be able to follow me better in what I have

Heat, once introduced into a chimney, rises. The rising air draws replacement from the lower opening. If a flame or smoke is near that opening it will be drawn downward and into the chimney. As long as the entering air continues to be heated, the process goes on.

to say hereafter. I suppose some here will have made for themselves the experiment I am going to show you. Am I right in supposing that any body here has played at snapdragon? I do not know a more beautiful illustration of the philosophy of flame, as to a certain part of its history, than the game of snapdragon. First, here is the dish; and let me say, that when you play snapdragon properly you ought to have the dish well warmed; you ought also to have warm plums and warm brandy, which however, I have not got. When you have put the spirit into the dish, you have the cup and the fuel; and are not the raisins acting like the wicks? I now throw the plums into the dish, and light the spirit, and you see those beautiful tongues of flame that I refer to. You have the air creeping in over the edge of the dish forming these tongues. Why? Because, through the force of the current and the irregularity of the action of the flame, it can not flow in one uniform stream. The air flows in so irregularly that you have what would otherwise be a single image broken up into a variety of forms, and each of these little tongues has an independent existence of its own. Indeed, I might say, you have here a multitude of independent candles. You must not imagine, because you see these tongues all at once, that the flame is of this particular shape.

A flame of that shape is never so at any one time. Never is a body of flame, like that which you just saw rising from the ball, of the shape it appears to you. It consists of a multitude of different shapes, succeeding each other so fast that the eye is only able to take cognizance of them all at once. In former times I purposely analyzed a flame of that general character, and the diagram shows you the different parts of which it is composed. They do not occur all at once; it is only because we see these shapes in such rapid succession that they seem to us to exist all at one time.

Lecture II

Air Necessary for Combustion—Brightness of the Flame—
The Products of the Combustion

We were occupied the last time we met in considering the
general character and arrangment as regards the fluid portion
of a candle, and the way in which that fluid got into the
place of combustion. You see, when we have a candle
burning fairly in a regular steady atmosphere, it will have a
shape something like the one shown in the diagram, and will
look pretty uniform, although very curious in its character.
And now I have to ask your attention to the means by which
we are enabled to ascertain what happens in any particular
part of the flame; why it happens; what it does in happening;
and where, after all, the whole candle goes to; because, as
you know very well, a candle being brought before us and
burned, disappears, if burned properly, without the least
trace of dirt in the candle stick; and this is a very curious cir-
cumstance. In order, then, to examine this candle carefully, I
have arranged a certain apparatus, the use of which you will
see as I go on. Here is a candle; I am about to put the end of
this glass tube into the middle of the flame—into that
part which was represented in the diagram as being rather
dark, and which you can see at any time if you will look

at a candle carefully, without blowing it about. We will examine this dark part first.

Now I take this bent glass tube, and introduce one end into that part of the flame, and you see at once that something is coming from the flame, out at the other end of the tube; and if I put a flask there, and leave it for a little while, you will see that something from the middle part of the flame is gradually drawn out, and goes through the tube and into that flask, and there behaves very differently from what it does in the open air. It not only escapes from the end of the tube, but falls down to the bottom of the flask like a heavy substance, as indeed it is. We find that this is the wax of the candle made into a vaporous fluid—not a gas. (You must learn the difference between a gas and a vapor; a gas remains permanent; a vapor is something that will condense.) If you blow out a candle, you perceive a very nasty smell, resulting from the condensation of this vapor. That is very different from what you have outside the flame; and, in order to make that more clear to you, I am about to produce and set fire to a larger portion of this vapor; for what we have in the small way in a candle we must produce in a larger way so that we may examine the different parts. And now Mr. Anderson will give me a source of heat, and I am about to show you what the vapor is. Here is some wax in a glass flask, and I am going to make it hot, as the inside of that candle-flame is hot, and the matter about the wick is hot. Now I dare say that is hot enough for me. You see that the wax I put in it has become fluid and there is a little smoke coming from it. We shall very soon have the vapor rising up. I will make it still hotter, and now we get more of it, so that I can actually pour the vapor out of the flask into that basin, and set it on fire there. This, then, is exactly the same kind of vapor as we have in the middle of the candle; and that you may be sure this is the case, let us try whether we have not got here, in this flask, a real combustible vapor out of the middle of the candle. See how it burns. Now this is the vapor from the middle of the

The vapor of a candle can be drawn off through a tube held in the dark part of the flame, just above the wick. This is where the wax is hot enough to vaporize, but where no air is causing it to burn.

EXPERIMENT 1, p. 85

15

"... there are clearly two different kinds of action—one of the production of the vapor, and the other the combustion of it— both of which take place in particular parts of the candle."

The piece of paper begins burning in the shape of a ring, indicating the area of greatest heat to be on the outside edge of the flame, where the air and fuel are combined.

EXPERIMENT 3, p. 88

candle, produced by its own heat; and that is one of the first things you have to consider with respect to the progress of the wax in the course of its combustion, and as regards the changes it undergoes. I will arrange another tube carefully in the flame, and I should not wonder if we were able, by a little care, to get that vapor to pass through the tube to the other extremity, where we will light it, and obtain absolutely the flame of the candle at a place distant from it. Now, look at that. Is not that a very pretty experiment? And you see from this that there are clearly two different kinds of action—one of the *production* of the vapor, and the other the *combustion* of it—both of which take place in particular parts of the candle.

I shall get no vapor from that part which is already burnt. If I raise the tube to the upper part of the flame, so soon as the vapor has been swept out what comes away will be no longer combustible; it is already burned. How burned? Why, burned thus: In the middle of the flame, where the wick is, there is this combustible vapor; on the outside of the flame is the air which we shall find necessary for the burning of the candle; between the two, intense chemical action takes place, whereby the air and the fuel act upon each other, and at the very same time that we obtain light the vapor inside is destroyed. If you examine where the heat of a candle is, you will find it very curiously arranged. Suppose I take this candle, and hold a piece of paper close upon the flame, where is the heat of that flame? Do you not see that it is *not* in the inside? It is in a ring, exactly in the place where I told you the chemical action was; and even in my irregular mode of making the experiment, if there is not too much disturbance, there will always be a ring. This is a good experiment for you to make at home. Take a strip of paper, have the air in the room quiet, and put the piece of paper right across the middle of the flame—(I must not talk while I make the experiment)—and you will find that it is burnt in two places, and that it is not burnt, or very little so, in the middle;

16

and when you have tried the experiment once or twice, so as to make it nicely, you will be very interested to see where the heat is, and to find that it is where the air and the fuel come together.

Air Necessary for Combustion

This is most important for us as we proceed with our subject. Air is absolutely necessary for combustion; and, what is more, I must have you understand that *fresh air* is necessary, or else we should be imperfect in our reasoning and our experiments. Here is a jar of air; I place it over a candle, and it burns very nicely in it at first, showing that what I have said about it is true; but there will soon be a change. See how the flame is drawing upward, presently fading, and at last going out. And going out, why? Not because it wants air merely, for the jar is as full now as it was before; but it wants pure, fresh air. The jar is full of air, partly changed, partly not changed; but it does not contain sufficient of the fresh air which is necessary for the combustion of a candle. If we look a little more closely into this kind of action, we shall find certain steps of reasoning extremely interesting. For instance, here is the oil-lamp I showed you—an excellent lamp for our experiments—the old Argand lamp. I now make it like a candle [obstructing the passage of air into the center of the flame]; there is the cotton; there is the oil rising up in it, and there is the conical flame. It burns poorly because there is a partial restraint of air. I have allowed no air to get to it save around the outside of the flame, and it does not burn well. I can not admit more air from the outside, because the wick is large; but if, as Argand did so cleverly, I open a passage to the middle of the flame, and so let air come in there, you will see how much more beautifully it burns. If I shut the air off, look how it smokes; and why? We have now some very interesting points to study: we have the case of the combustion of a candle; we have the case of a candle being put out by the

The jar is full of air but not of a sufficient quantity of the fresh air necessary for combustion.

EXPERIMENT 4, p. 89

By jar, Faraday here means a bell jar, one open at the bottom and closed at the top like a bell.

An Argand Lamp has a tubular wick which admits a current of air inside the flame, as well as outside of it, causing more complete combustion.

want of air; and we have now the case of imperfect combustion, and this is to us so interesting that I want you to understand it as thoroughly as you do the case of a candle burning in its best possible manner. I will now make a great flame, because we need the largest possible illustrations. Here is a larger wick (burning turpentine on a ball of cotton). All these things are the same as candles, after all. If we have larger wicks, we must have a larger supply of air, or we shall have less perfect combustion. Look, now, at this black substance going up into the atmosphere; there is a regular stream of it. I have provided means to carry off the imperfectly-burned part, lest it should annoy you. Look at the soots that fly off from the flame; see what an imperfect combustion it is, because it can not get enough air. What, then, is happening? Why, certain things which are necessary to the combustion of a candle are absent, and very bad results are accordingly produced; but we see what happens to a candle when it is burnt in a pure and proper state of air. At the time when I showed you this charring by the ring of flame on the one side of the paper, I might have also shown you, by turning to the other side, that the burning of a candle produces the same kind of soot—charcoal, or carbon.

EXPERIMENT 3, p. 88
EXPERIMENT 5, p. 90

But, before I show that, let me explain to you, as it is quite necessary for our purpose, that, though I take a candle, and give you, as the general result, its combustion in the form of a flame, we must see whether combustion is always in this condition, or whether there are other conditions of flame; and we shall soon discover that there are, and that they are most important to us. I think, perhaps, the best illustration of such a point to us is to show the result of strong contrast. Here is a little gunpowder. You know that gunpowder burns with flame; we may fairly call it flame. It contains carbon and other materials, which altogether cause it to burn with a flame. And here is some pulverized iron, or iron filings. Now I purpose burning these two things together. I have a little mortar in which I will mix them. (Before I go

into these experiments, let me hope that none of you, by trying to repeat them for fun's sake, will do any harm. These things may all be very properly used if you take care, but without that much mischief will be done.) Well, then, here is a little gunpowder, which I put at the bottom of that little wooden vessel, and mix the iron filings up with it, my object being to make the gunpowder set fire to the filings and burn them in the air, and thereby show the difference between substances burning with flame and not with flame. Here is the mixture; and when I set fire to it you must watch the combustion, and you will see that it is of two kinds. You will see the gunpowder burning with a flame and the filings thrown up. You will see them burning, too, but without the production of flame. They will each burn separately. There is the gunpowder, which burns with a flame, and there are the filings: they burn with a different kind of combustion. You see, then, these two great distinctions; and upon these differences depend all the utility and all the beauty of flame which we use for the purpose of giving out light. When we use oil, or gas, or candle for the purpose of illumination, their fitness all depends upon these different kinds of combustion.

The gunpowder and iron filings each burn separately and with a different kind of combustion.

There are such curious conditions of flame that it requires some cleverness and nicety of discrimination to distinguish the kinds of combustion one from another. For instance, here is a powder which is very combustible, consisting as you see, of separate little particles. It is called *lycopodium*, and each of these particles can produce a vapor, and produce its own flame; but, to see them burning, you would imagine it was all one flame. I will now set fire to a quantity, and you will see the effect. We saw a cloud of flame, apparently in one body; but that rushing noise was a proof that the combustion was not a continuous or regular one. This is the lightning of the pantomimes, and a very good imitation. This is not an example of combustion like that of the filings I have been speaking of, to which we must now return.

Lycopodium is a fine, yellowish powder composed of the spores of the club moss.

Suppose I take a candle and examine that part of it which

19

appears brightest to our eyes. Why, there I get these black particles, which already you have seen many times evolved from the flame, and which I am now about to evolve in a different way. I will take this candle and clear away the gutterage, which occurs by reason of the currents of air; and if I now arrange the glass tube so as just to dip into this luminous part, as in our first experiment, only higher, you see the result. In place of having the same white vapor that you had before, you will now have a black vapor. There it goes, as black as ink. It is certainly very different from the white vapor; and when we put a light to it we shall find that it does not burn, but that it puts the light out. Well, these particles, as I said before, are just the smoke of the candle; and this brings to mind that old employment which Dean Swift recommended to servants for their amusement, namely, writing on the ceiling of a room with a candle. But what is that black substance? Why, it is the same carbon which exists in the candle. How comes it out of the candle? It evidently existed in the candle, or else we should not have had it here. And now I want you to follow me in this explanation. You would hardly think that all those substances which fly about London, in the form of soots and blacks, are the very beauty and life of the flame, and which are burned in it as those iron filings were burned here. Here is a piece of wire gauze, which will not let the flame go through it, and I think you will see, almost immediately, that when I bring it low enough to touch that part of the flame which is otherwise so bright, it quells and quenches it at once, and allows a volume of smoke to rise up.

Brightness of the Flame

I want you now to follow me in this point—that whenever a substance burns, as the iron filings burnt in the flame of gunpowder, without assuming the vaporous state (whether it becomes liquid or remains solid), it becomes exceedingly luminous. I have here taken three or four examples apart

Davy Mine Lamp

The wire gauze (screen) prevents the flame passing through it, causing imperfect combustion. EXPERIMENT 5, p. 90

The Davy Lamp was a miner's lamp constructed with a view to avoiding explosions in an atmosphere containing inflammable gas. In the most common form, the flame is enclosed by fine wire screen which, through its cooling effect, prevents the flame from passing.

from the candle on purpose to illustrate this point to you, because what I have to say is applicable to all substances, whether they burn or whether they do not burn—that they are exceedingly bright if they retain their solid state, and that it is to this presence of solid particles in the candle-flame that it owes it brilliancy.

Here is a platinum wire, a body which does not change by heat. If I heat it in this flame, see how exceedingly luminous it becomes. I will make the flame dim for the purpose of giving a little light only, and yet you will see that the heat which it can give to that platinum wire, though far less than the heat it has itself, is able to raise the platinum wire to a far higher state of effulgence. This flame has carbon in it; but I will take one that has no carbon in it. There is a material—a kind of fuel—a vapor or gas, whichever you like to call it—in that vessel, and it has no solid particles in it; so I take that because it is an example of flame itself burning without any solid matter whatever; and if I now put this solid substance in it, you see what an intense heat it has, and how brightly it causes the solid body to glow. This is the pipe through which we convey this particular gas, which we call hydrogen, and which you shall know all about the next time we meet. And here is a substance called oxygen, by means of which this hydrogen can burn; and although we produce, by their mixture, far greater heat than you can obtain from the candle, yet there is very little light. If, however, I take a solid substance, and put that into it, we produce an intense light. If I take a piece of lime, a substance which will not burn, and which will not vaporize by the heat (and because it does not vaporize remains solid, and remains heated), you will soon observe what happens as to its glowing. I have here a most intense heat produced by the burning of hydrogen in contact with the oxygen; but there is as yet very little light—not for want of heat, but for want of particles which can retain their solid state; but when I hold this piece of lime in the flame of the hydrogen as it burns in the oxygen, see how it glows! This

Bunsen calculated the temperature of the oxy-hydrogen blowpipe to be 8061° Centigrade. Hydrogen burning in air has a temperature of 3259° Centigrade.

Limelight is an intense light produced by the incandescence of a stick or ball of lime in the flame of a combination of oxygen and hydrogen gases or of oxygen and coal gas. Limelight is also called calcium light or Drummond light.

EXPERIMENT 6, p. 92

The sulphuric acid inflames the mixture of sulphuret of antimony and chlorate of potassa. A portion of the chlorate of potassa is decomposed by the sulphuric acid into oxide of chlorine, bisulphate of potassa, and perchlorate of potassa. The oxide of chlorine inflames the sulphuret of antimony, which is a combustible body, and the whole mass instantly bursts into flame. (Faraday)

is the glorious lime light, which rivals the voltaic light, and which is almost equal to sunlight. I have here a piece of carbon or charcoal, which will burn and give us light exactly in the same manner as if it were burnt as part of a candle. The heat that is in the flame of a candle decomposes the vapor of the wax, and sets free the carbon particles; they rise up heated and glowing as this now glows, and then enter into the air. But the particles, when burnt, never pass off from a candle in the form of carbon. They go off into the air as a perfectly invisible substance, about which we shall know hereafter.

Is it not beautiful to think that such a process is going on, and that such a dirty thing as charcoal can become so incandescent? You see it comes to this—that all bright flames contain these solid particles; all things that burn and produce solid particles, either during the time they are burning, as in the candle, or immediately after being burnt, as in the case of the gunpowder and iron filings—all these things give us this glorious and beautiful light.

I will give you a few illustrations. Here is a piece of phosphorus, which burns with a bright flame. Very well; we may now conclude that phosphorus will produce, either at the moment that it is burning or afterwards, these solid particles. Here is the phosphorus lighted, and I cover it over with this glass for the purpose of keeping in what is produced. What is all that smoke? That smoke consists of those very particles which are produced by the combustion of the phosphorus. Here again are two substances. This is chlorate of potassa, and this other sulphuret of antimony. I shall mix these together a little, and then they may be burnt in many ways. I shall touch them with a drop of sulphuric acid, for the purpose of giving you an illustration of chemical action, and they will instantly burn. Now, from the appearance of things, you can judge for yourselves whether they produce solid matter in burning. I have given you the train of reasoning which will enable you to say whether they do or do not; for

22

what is this bright flame but the solid particles passing off?

Mr. Anderson has in the furnace a very hot crucible. I am about to throw into it some zinc filings, and they will burn with a flame like gunpowder. I make this experiment because you can make it well at home. Now I want you to see what will be the result of the combustion of this zinc. Here it is burning—burning beautifully like a candle, I may say. But what is all that smoke, and what are those little clouds of wool which will come to you . . . in the form of the old philosophic wool, as it was called. We shall have left in that crucible, also, a quantity of this woolly matter. But I will take a piece of this same zinc, and make an experiment a little more closely at home, as it were. You will have here the same thing happening. Here is the piece of zinc; there [indicates a jet of hydrogen] is the furnace, and we will set to work and try and burn the metal. It glows, you see; there is the combustion; and there is the white substance into which it burns. And so, if I take that flame of hydrogen as the representative of a candle, and show you a substance like zinc burning in the flame, you will see that it was merely during the action of combustion that this substance glowed—while it was kept hot; and if I take a flame of hydrogen and put this white substance from the zinc into it, look how beautifully it glows, and just because it is a solid substance.

I will now take such a flame as I had a moment since, and set free from it the particles of carbon. Here is some camphene, which will burn with a smoke; but if I send these particles of smoke through this pipe into the hydrogen flame you will see they will burn and become luminous, because we heat them a second time. There they are. Those are the particles of carbon reignited a second time. They are those particles which you can easily see by holding a piece of paper behind them, and which, while they are in the flame, are ignited by the heat produced, and, when so ignited, produce this brightness. When the particles are not

Philosophic wool, or flowers of zinc, is the oxidized vapor of zinc which has cooled to a fluffy, powdery solid. EXPERIMENT 7, p. 94

EXPERIMENT 8, p. 96

Camphene is a rectified oil of turpentine that was commonly used in lamps.

23

Coal-gas is gas made from coal; specifically that made by distilling bituminous coal in retorts and used for lighting and heating. It consists chiefly of hydrogen and methane, with small amounts of carbon monoxide, nitrogen, ethylene, etc.

separated you get no brightness. The flame of coal-gas owes its brightness to the separation, during combustion, of these particles of carbon, which are equally in that as in a candle. I can very quickly alter that arrangement. Here, for instance, is a bright flame of gas. Supposing I add so much air to the flame as to cause it all to burn before those particles are set free, I shall not have this brightness; and I can do that in this way: If I place over the jet this wire-gauze cap, as you see, and then light the gas over it, it burns with a non-luminous flame, owing to its having plenty of air mixed with it before it burns; and if I raise the gauze, you see it does not burn below. There is plenty of carbon in the gas; but, because the atmosphere can get to it, and mix with it before it burns, you see how pale and blue the flame is. And if I blow upon a bright gas-flame, so as to consume all this carbon before it gets heated to the glowing point, it will also burn blue. The only reason why I have not the same bright light when I thus blow upon the flame is that the carbon meets with sufficient air to burn it before it gets separated in the flame in a free state. The difference is solely due to the solid particles not being separated before the gas is burnt.

Products of the Combustion

You observe that there are certain products as the result of the combustion of a candle and that of these products one portion may be considered as charcoal, or soot; that charcoal, when afterward burnt, produces some other product; and it concerns us very much now to ascertain what that other product is. . . . Now there is going through this tube all the products of that candle, and you will presently see that the tube will become quite opaque. Suppose I take another candle, and place it under a jar, and then put a light on the other side, just to show you what is going on. You see that the sides of the jar become cloudy, and the light begins to burn feebly. It is the products, you see, which make the light so dim, and this is the same thing which makes the sides

of the jar so opaque. If you go home, and take a spoon that has been in the cold air, and hold it over a candle—not so as to soot it—you will find that it becomes dim just as that jar is dim. If you can get a silver dish, or something of that kind, you will make the experiment still better; and now, just to carry your thoughts forward to the time we shall next meet, let me tell you that it is *water* which causes the dimness, and when we next meet I will show you that we can make it, without difficulty, assume the form of a liquid.

Lecture III

Products: Water from the Combustion—Nature of Water—
A Compound—Hydrogen

Products of Combustion of the Candle

I dare say you well remember that when we parted we had
just mentioned the word "products" from the candle; for
when a candle burns we found we were able, by nice adjust-
ment, to get various products from it. There was one
substance which was not obtained when the candle was
burning properly, which was charcoal or smoke, and there
was some other substance that went upward from the flame
which did not appear as smoke, but took some other form,
and made part of that general current which, ascending from
the candle upward, becomes invisible, and escapes. There
were also other products to mention. You remember that in
that rising current having its origin at the candle we found
that one part was condensable against a cold spoon, or
against a clean plate, or any other cold thing, and another
part was incondensable.

Water from the Combustion

We will first take the condensable part, and examine it,
and, strange to say, we find that that part of the product is

just water—nothing but water. On the last occasion I spoke of it incidentally, merely saying that water was produced among the condensable products of the candle; but to-day I wish to draw your attention to water, that we may examine it carefully, especially in relation to this subject, and also with respect to its general existence on the surface of the globe.

The Nature of Water

Now, having previously arranged an experiment for the purpose of condensing water from the products of the candle, my next point will be to show you this water; and perhaps one of the best means that I can adopt for showing its presence to so many at once is to exhibit a very visible action of water, and then to apply that test to what is collected as a drop at the bottom of that vessel. I have here a chemical substance, discovered by Sir Humphrey Davy, which has a very energetic action upon water, which I shall use as a test of the presence of water. If I take a little piece of it—it is called potassium, as coming from potash—if I take a little piece of it, and throw it into that basin, you see how it shows the presence of water by lighting up and floating about, burning with a violet flame. I am now going to take away the candle which has been burning beneath the vessel containing ice and salt, and you see a drop of water—a condensed product of the candle—hanging from the under surface of the dish. I will show you that potassium has the same action upon it as upon the water in that basin in the experiment we have just tried. See! it takes fire, and burns in just the same manner. I will take another drop upon this glass slab, and when I put the potassium on to it, you see at once, from its taking fire, that there is water present. Now that water was produced by the candle. In the same manner, if I put this spirit-lamp under that jar, you will soon see the latter become damp from the dew which is deposited upon it— that dew being the result of combustion; and I have no doubt you will shortly see, by the drops of water which fall upon

Potassium was discovered by Faraday's teacher, Sir Humphrey Davy, in 1807 when he succeeded in separating it from potash by means of a voltaic pile.

The water condensing on the outside of the cold flask is a product of combustion.
EXPERIMENT 9, p. 97

the paper below, that there is a good deal of water produced from the combustion of the lamp. I will let it remain, and you can afterward see how much water has been collected. So, if I take a gas-lamp, and put any cooling arrangement over it, I shall get water—water being likewise produced from the combustion of gas. Here, in this bottle, is a quantity of water—perfectly pure, distilled water, produced from the combustion of a gas-lamp—in no point different from the water that you distill from the river, or ocean, or spring, but exactly the same thing. Water is one individual thing; it never changes. We can add to it by careful adjustment for a little while, or we can take it apart and get other things from it; but water, as water, remains always the same, either in a solid, liquid, or fluid state. Here again is some water produced by the combustion of an oil-lamp. A pint of oil, when burnt fairly and properly, produces rather more than a pint of water. Here, again, is some water, produced by a rather long experiment, from a wax candle. And so we can go on with almost all combustible substances, and find that if they burn with a flame, as a candle, they produce water. You may make these experiments yourselves: the head of a poker is a very good thing to try with, and if it remains cold long enough over the candle, you may get water condensed in drops on it; or a spoon, or ladle, or any thing else may be used, provided it be clean, and can carry off the heat, and so condense the water.

And now—to go into the history of this wonderful production of water from combustibles, and by combustion—I must first of all tell you that this water may exist in different conditions; and although you may now be acquainted with all its forms, they still require us to give a little attention to them for the present; so that we may perceive how the water, while it goes through its Protean changes, is entirely and absolutely the same thing, whether it is produced from a candle, by combustion, or from the rivers or ocean.

The word Protean, meaning exceedingly variable, comes from the name of Proteus, a Greek sea god who could assume many different shapes.

28

Water—A Compound

First of all, water when at the coldest, is ice. Now we philosophers—I hope that I may class you and myself together in this case—speak of water as water, whether it be in its solid, or liquid, or gaseous state—we speak of it chemically as water. Water is a thing compounded of two substances, one of which we have derived from the candle, and the other we shall find elsewhere. Water may occur as ice. . . . Ice changes back into water when the temperature is raised; water also changes into steam when it is warmed enough. The water which we have here before us is in its densest state (at 39.1°F.); and, although it changes in weight, in condition, in form, and in many other qualities, it still is water; and whether we alter it into ice by cooling, or whether we change it into steam by heat, it increases in volume —in the one case very strangely and powerfully, and in the other case very largely and wonderfully. For instance, I will now take this thin cylinder, and pour a little water into it, and, seeing how much water I pour in, you may easily estimate for yourselves how high it will rise in the vessel: it will cover the bottom about two inches. I am now about to convert the water into steam for the purpose of showing to you the different volumes which water occupies in its different states of water and steam.

Let us now take the case of water changing into ice: we can effect that by cooling it in a mixture of salt and pounded ice—and I shall do so to show you the expansion of water into a thing of larger bulk when it is so changed. These bottles are made of strong cast iron, very strong and very thick—I suppose they are the third of an inch in thickness; they are very carefully filled with water, so as to exclude all air, and then they are screwed down tight. We shall see that when we freeze the water in these iron vessels, they will not be able to hold the ice, and the expansion within them will break them in pieces as these are broken, which have been

A mixture of salt and pounded (crushed) ice reduces the temperature from 32° F. to zero, the ice at the same time becoming liquid.

bottles of exactly the same kind. I am about to put these two bottles into that mixture of ice and salt for the purpose of showing that when water becomes ice it changes in volume in this extraordinary way.

In the mean time, look at the change which has taken place in the water to which we have applied heat; it is losing its fluid state. You may tell this by two or three circumstances. I have covered the mouth of this glass flask, in which water is boiling, with a watch-glass. Do you see what happens? It rattles away like a valve chattering, because the steam rising from the boiling water sends the valve up and down, and forces itself out, and so makes it clatter. You can very easily perceive that the flask is quite full of steam, or else it would not force its way out. You see also that the flask contains a substance very much larger than the water, for it fills the whole of the flask over and over again, and there it is blowing away into the air; and yet you can not observe any great diminution in the bulk of the water, which shows you that its change in bulk is very great when it becomes steam.

Tightly-capped iron bottles, filled with water and set aside to freeze, will burst due to the expansion of water when it becomes a solid.

EXPERIMENT 10, p. 99

I have put our iron bottles containing water into this freezing mixture, that you may see what happens. No communication will take place, you observe, between the water in the bottles and the ice in the outer vessel. But there will be a conveyance of heat from the one to the other, and if we are successful—we are making our experiment in very great haste—I expect you will by-and-by, so soon as the cold has taken possession of the bottles and their contents, hear a pop on the occasion of the bursting of one bottle or the other, and, when we come to examine the bottles, we shall find their contents masses of ice, partly inclosed by the covering of iron which is too small for them, because the ice is larger in bulk than the water. You know very well that ice floats upon water; if a boy falls through a hole in the water, he tries to get on the ice again to float him up. Why does the ice float? Think of that, and philosophize. Because the ice is larger than the quantity of water which can produce it, and

therefore the ice weighs the lighter and the water is the heavier.

To return now to the action of heat on water. See what a stream of vapor is issuing from this tin vessel. You observe, we must have made it quite full of steam to have it sent out in that great quantity. And now, as we can convert the water into steam by heat, we convert it back into liquid by the application of cold. And if we take a glass, or any other cold thing, and hold it over this steam, see how soon it gets damp with water: it will condense it until the glass is warm—it condenses the water which is now running down the sides of it. I have here another experiment to show the condensation of water from a vaporous state back into a liquid state, in the same way as the vapor, one of the products of the candle, was condensed against the bottom of the dish and obtained in the form of water; and to show you how truly and thoroughly these changes take place, I will take this tin flask, which is now full of steam, and close the top. We shall see what takes place when we cause this water or steam to return back to the fluid state by pouring some cold water on the outside. You see what has happened. If I had closed the stopper, and still kept the heat applied to it, it would have burst the vessel; yet, when the steam returns to the state of water, the vessel collapses, there being a vacuum produced inside by the condensation of the steam. I show you these experiments for the purpose of pointing out that in all these occurrences there is nothing that changes the water into any other thing; it still remains water; and so the vessel is obliged to give way, and is crushed inward, as in the other case, by the farther application of heat, it would have been blown outward.

And what do you think the bulk of that water is when it assumes the vaporous condition? You see that cube (1 cubic foot). There, by its side, is a cubic inch, exactly the same shape as the cubic foot, and that bulk of water (1 cubic inch) is sufficient to expand into that bulk (1 cubic foot) of steam;

The metal vessel, which was filled with steam before it was tightly capped, collapses when the water poured on the outside condenses the steam back to water. EXPERIMENT 11, p. 100

One cubic foot of steam equals one cubic inch of water.

31

and, on the contrary, the application of cold will contract that large quantity of steam into this small quantity of water. Ah! There is one of our bottles burst, and here, you see, is a crack down one side an eighth of an inch in width. This other bottle is also broken; although the iron was nearly half an inch thick, the ice has burst it asunder. These changes always take place in water; they do not require to be always produced by artificial means; we only use them here because we want to produce a small winter round that little bottle instead of a long and severe one. But if you go to Canada, or to the North, you will find the temperature there out of doors will do the same thing as has been done here by the freezing mixture.

To return to our quiet philosophy. We shall not in future be deceived, therefore, by any changes that are produced in water. Water is the same every where, whether produced from the ocean or from the flame of the candle. Where, then, is this water which we get from a candle? I must anticipate a little, and tell you. It evidently comes, as to part of it, from the candle, but is it within the candle beforehand? No, it is not in the candle; and it is not in the air around about the candle which is necessary for its combustion. It is neither in one nor the other, but it comes from their conjoint action, a part from the candle, a part from the air; and this we have now to trace, so that we may understand thoroughly what is the chemical history of a candle when we have it burning on our table. How shall we get at this? I myself know plenty of ways, but I want *you* to get at it from the association in your own minds of what I have already told you.

I think you can see a little in this way. We had just now the case of a substance which acted upon the water in the way that Sir Humphrey Davy showed us, and which I am now going to recall to your minds by making again an experiment upon that dish. It is a thing which we have to handle very carefully; for you see, if I allow a little splash of water to come upon this mass, it sets fire to part of it; and if there

were free access of air, it would quickly set fire to the whole. Now this is a metal—a beautiful and bright metal—which rapidly changes in the air, and, as you know, rapidly changes in water. I will put a piece on the water, and you see it burns beautifully, making a floating lamp, using the water in the place of air. Again, if we take a few iron filings or turnings and put them in water, we find that they likewise undergo an alteration. They do not change so much as this potassium does, but they change somewhat in the same way; they become rusty, and show an action upon the water, though in a different degree of intensity to what this beautiful metal does; but they act upon the water in the same manner generally as this potassium. I want you to put these different facts together in your minds. I have another metal here (zinc), and when we examined it with regard to the solid substance produced by its combustion, we had an opportunity of seeing that it burned; and I suppose, if I take a little strip of this zinc and put it over the candle, you will see something half way, as it were, between the combustion of potassium on the water and the action of iron—you see there is a sort of combustion. It has burned, leaving a white ash or residuum; and here also we find that the metal has a certain amount of action upon water.

By degrees we have learned how to modify the action of these different substances, and to make them tell us what we want to know. And now, first of all, I take iron. It is a common thing in all chemical reactions, where we get any result of this kind, to find that it is increased by the action of heat; and if we want to examine minutely and carefully the action of bodies one upon another, we often have to refer to the action of heat. You are aware, I believe, that iron filings burn beautifully in the air; but I am about to show you an experiment of this kind, because it will impress upon you what I am going to say about iron in its action on water. If I take a flame and make it hollow—you know why, because I want to get air to it and into it, and therefore I make it hol-

Potassium has a great chemical affinity for oxygen; this causes it to decompose water to produce hydrogen, which ignites in the heat produced by the reaction.

EXPERIMENT 7, p. 94

33

low—and then take a few iron filings and drop them into the flame, you see how well they burn. That combustion results from the chemical action which is going on when we ignite those particles. And so we proceed to consider these different effects, and ascertain what iron will do when it meets with water. It will tell us the story so beautifully, so gradually and regularly, that I think it will please you very much.

I have here a furnace with a pipe going through it like an iron gun-barrel, and I have stuffed that barrel full of bright iron turnings, and placed it across the fire to be made red-hot. We can either send air through the barrel to come in contact with the iron, or we can send steam from this little boiler at the end of the barrel. Here is a stopcock which shuts off the steam from the barrel until we wish to admit it. There is some water in these glass jars, which I have colored blue, so that you may see what happens. Now you know very well that any steam I might send through the barrel, if it went through into the water, would be condensed; for you have seen that steam can not retain its gaseous form if it be cooled down; you saw it here crushing itself into a small bulk, and causing the flask holding it to collapse; so that if I were to send steam through that barrel it would be condensed, supposing the barrel were cold; it is therefore heated to perform the experiment I am now about to show you. I am going to send the steam through the barrel in small quantities, and you shall judge for yourselves, when you see it issue from the other end, whether it still remains steam. Steam is condensible into water, and when you lower the temperature of steam you convert it back into fluid water; but I have lowered the temperature of the gas which I have collected in this jar by passing it through water after it has traversed the iron barrel, and still it does not change back into water. I will take another test and apply to this gas. (I hold the jar in an inverted position, or my substance would escape.) If I now apply a light to the mouth of the jar, it ignites with a slight noise. That tells you that it is not steam;

The apparatus which Faraday used to "crack" steam and release a gas. The iron filings, when hot, readily react with part of the water vapor, forming a new iron compound.

steam puts out a fire: it does not burn; but you saw that what I had in that jar burnt. We may obtain this substance equally from water produced from the candle flame as from any other source. When it is obtained by the action of the iron upon the aqueous vapor, it leaves the iron in a state very similar to that in which these filings were after they were burnt. It makes the iron heavier than it was before. So long as the iron remains in the tube and is heated, and is cooled again without the access of air or water, it does not change its weight; but after having had this current of steam passed over it, it them comes out heavier than it was before, and having taken something out of the steam, and having allowed something else to pass forth, which we see here. And now, as we have another jar full, I will show you something most interesting. It is a combustible gas; and I might at once take this jar and set fire to the contents, and show you that it is combustible; but I intend to show you more, if I can. It is also a very light substance. Steam will condense; this body will rise in the air, and not condense. Suppose I take another glass jar, empty of all but air: if I examine it with a taper I shall find that it contains nothing but air. I will now take this jar full of the gas that I am speaking of, and deal with it as

The invisible light gas, here represented, can be poured just like a liquid —only upside-down.

"There is something coming off from the zinc very abundantly, which is not steam."

though it were a light body; I will hold both upside down, and turn the one up under the other; and that which did contain the gas procured from the steam, what does it contain now? You will find it now only contains air. But look! Here is the combustible substance which I have poured out of the one jar into the other. It still preserves its quality, and condition, and independence, and therefore is the more worthy of our consideration, as belonging to the products of a candle.

Now this substance which we have just prepared by the action of iron on the steam or water, we can also get by means of those other things which you have already seen act so well upon the water. If I take a piece of potassium, and make the necessary arrangements, it will produce this gas; and if instead a piece of zinc, I find, when I come to examine it very carefully, that the main reason why this zinc can not act upon the water continuously as the other metal does is because the result of the action of the water envelops the zinc in a kind of protecting coat. We have learned in consequence, that if we put into our vessel only the zinc and water, they, by themselves, do not give rise to much action, and we get no result. But suppose I proceed to dissolve off this varnish—this encumbering substance—which I can do by a little acid; the moment I do this I find the zinc acting upon the water exactly as the iron did, but at the common temperature. The acid in no way is altered except in its combination with the oxide of zinc which is produced. I have now poured the acid into the glass, and the effect is as though I were to apply heat to cause this boiling up. There is something coming off from the zinc very abundantly, which is not steam. There is a jar full of it; and you will find that I have exactly the same combustible substance remaining in the vessel, when I hold it upside down, that I produced during the experiment with the iron barrel. This is what we get from water, the same substance which is contained in the candle.

36

Hydrogen

Let us now trace distinctly the connection between these two points. This is hydrogen—a body classed among those things which in chemistry we call elements, because we can get nothing else out of them. A candle is not an elementary body, because we can get carbon out of it; we can get this hydrogen out of it, or at least out of the water which it supplies. And this gas has been so named hydrogen, because it is that element which, in association with another, generates water. Mr. Anderson having now been able to get two or three jars of gas, we shall have a few experiments to make, and I want to show you the best way of making these experiments, if you will only make them with care and attention, and the assent of those around you. As we advance in chemistry we are obliged to deal with substances which are rather injurious if in their wrong places; the acids, and heat, and combustible things we use might do harm if carelessly employed. If you want to make hydrogen, you can make it easily from bits of zinc, and sulphuric or muriactic acid. Here is what in former times was called the "philosopher's candle." It is a little phial with a cork and a tube or pipe passing through it. And I am now putting a few little pieces of zinc into it. This little instrument I am going to apply to a useful purpose in our demonstrations, for I want to show you that you can prepare hydrogen, and make some experiments with it as you please, at your own homes. Let me here tell you why I am so careful to fill this phial nearly, and yet not quite full. I do it because the evolved gas, which, as you have seen, is very combustible, is explosive to a considerable extent when mixed with air, and might lead to harm if you were to apply a light to the end of that pipe before all the air had been swept out of the space above the water. I am now about to pour in the sulphuric acid. I have used very little zinc and more sulphuric acid and water, because I want to keep it at work for some time. I therefore take care in this way to modify the proportions of the ingredients so that I

The term hydrogen comes from the Greek words "hydra" and "genes" meaning "Water-producer."

EXPERIMENT 12, p. 101

37

The philosopher's candle. Faraday was careful to test the gas before lighting it from the tube, as hydrogen mixed with air is highly explosive.

As the lecturer blew the bubbles with hydrogen, they rose, of course, high into the domed roof of the Royal Institution's Lecture Theatre.

may have a regular supply—not too quick and not too slow. Supposing I now take a glass and put it upside down over the end of the tube, because the hydrogen is light I expect that it will remain in that vessel a little while. We will now test the contents of our glass to see if there be hydrogen in it; I think I am safe in saying we have caught some. There it is, you see. I will now apply a light to the top of the tube. There is the hydrogen burning. There is our philosophical candle. It is a foolish, feeble sort of a flame, you may say, but it is so hot that scarcely any common flame gives out so much heat. It goes on burning regularly, and I am now about to put that flame to burn under a certain arrangement, in order that we may examine its results and make use of the information which we may thereby acquire. Inasmuch as the candle produces water, and this gas comes out of the water, let us see what this gives us by the same process of combustion that the candle went through when it burnt in the atmosphere, and for that purpose I am going to put the lamp under this apparatus, in order to condense whatever may arise from the combustion within it. In the course of a short time you will see moisture appearing in the cylinder, and you will get the water running down the side, and the water from this hydrogen flame will have absolutely the same effect upon all our tests, being obtained by the same general process as in the former case. This hydrogen is a very beautiful substance. It is so light that it carries things up; it is far lighter than the atmosphere, and I dare say I can show you this by an experiment which, if you are very clever, some of you may even have skill enough to repeat. Here is our generator of hydrogen, and here are some soapsuds. I have an India-rubber tube connected with the hydrogen generator, and at the end of the tube is a tobacco-pipe. I can thus put the pipe into the suds and blow bubbles by means of the hydrogen. You observe how the bubbles fall downward when I blow them with my warm breath; but notice the difference when I blow them with hydrogen.

It shows you how light this gas must be in order to carry with it not merely the ordinary soap-bubble, but the larger portion of a drop hanging to the bottom of it. I can show its lightness in a better way than this; larger bubbles than these may be so lifted up; indeed, in former times balloons used to be filled with this gas. Mr. Anderson will fasten this tube on to our generator, and we shall have a stream of hydrogen here with which we can charge this balloon made of collodion. I need not even be very careful to get all the air out, for I know the power of this gas to carry it up. Here is another larger one, made of thin membrane, which we will fill and allow to ascend; you will see they will all remain floating about until the gas escapes.

Collodion is a sticky liquid consisting of a mixture of alcohol and ether in which soluble guncotton or pyrozylin is dissolved. On evaporation of the solvents the pyrozylin remains in a tough adhesive form which was used as a coating for wounds and as an emulsion for photographic films.

	Pint	Ft3
Hydrogen	3/4 gr.	1/12 oz.
Water	8,750 gr.	1000 oz.

What, then, are the comparative weights of these substances? I have a table here which will show you the proportion which their weights bear to each other. I have taken a pint and a cubic foot as the measures, and have placed opposite to them the respective figures. A pint measure of this hydrogen weighs three quarters of our smallest weight, a grain, and a cubic foot weighs one twelfth of an ounce; whereas a pint of water weighs 8750 grains, and a cubic foot of water weighs almost 1000 ounces. You see, therefore, what a vast difference there is between the weight of a cubic foot of water and a cubic foot of hydrogen.

Hydrogen gives rise to no substance that can become solid, either during combustion or afterward as a product of its combustion; but when it burns it produces water only; and if we take a cold glass and put it over the flame, it becomes damp, and you have water produced immediately in

A voltaic pile is a battery constructed by piling up alternating series of two dissimilar metals, such as copper and zinc, with disks of cloth or paper between them. The cloth or paper disks were moistened with acid water and an electric current then ran through the battery. The power of current was in proportion to the area and number of disks employed.
EXPERIMENT 13, p. 103

Faraday here made contact between the two terminals of the battery, producing a brilliant flash of light.

This is similar to a modern electric welding unit.

appreciable quantity; and nothing is produced by its combustion but the same water which you have seen the flame of the candle produce. It is important to remember that this hydrogen is the only thing in nature which furnishes water as the sole product of combustion.

And now we must endeavor to find some additional proof of the general character and composition of water, and for this purpose I will keep you a little longer, so that at our next meeting we may be better prepared for the subject. We have the power of arranging the zinc which you have seen acting upon the water by the assistance of an acid, in such a manner as to cause all the power to be evolved in the place where we require it. I have behind me a voltaic pile, and I am just about to show you, at the end of this lecture, its character and power, that you may see what we shall have to deal with when next we meet. I hold here the extremities of the wires which transport the power from behind me, and which I shall cause to act on the water.

We have previously seen what a power of combustion is possessed by the potassium, or the zinc, or the iron filings; but none of them show such energy as this. This light is, in fact, produced by a forty-zinc power of burning; it is a power that I can carry about in my hands through these wires at pleasure, although if I applied it wrongly to myself it would destroy me in an instant, for it is a most intense thing, and the power you see here put forth while you count five is equivalent to the power of several thunder-storms, so great is its force. And that you may see what intense energy it has, I will take the ends of the wires which convey the power from the battery, and with it I dare say I can burn this iron file. Now this is a chemical power, and one which, when we next meet, I shall apply to water, and show you what results we are able to produce.

Lecture IV

Hydrogen in the Candle—Burns into Water—The Other Part
of Water—Oxygen

Hydrogen in the Candle—Burns into Water
When our candle was burning we found it produced water
exactly like the water we have around us; and by farther
examination of this water we found in it that curious body,
hydrogen—that light substance of which there is some in this
jar. We afterward saw the burning powers of that hydrogen,
and that it produced water. And I think I introduced to your
notice an apparatus which I very briefly said was an ar-
rangement of chemical force, or power, or energy, so
adjusted as to convey its power to us in these wires; and I
said I should use that force to pull the water to pieces, to see
what else there was in the water besides hydrogen; because,
you remember, when we passed the water through the iron
tube, we by no means got the weight of water back which we
put in in the form of steam, though we had a very large
quantity of gas evolved. We have now to see what is the
other substance present. That you may understand the char-
acter and use of this instrument, let us make an experiment
or two. Let us put together, first of all, some substances,
knowing what they are, and then see what the instrument

EXPERIMENT 14, p. 104

The gases given off at
the two electrodes are
collected together by
displacement of water in
the jar [F].

does to them. There is some copper (observe the various changes which it can undergo), and here is some nitric acid, and you will find that this, being a strong chemical agent, will act very powerfully when I add it to the copper. It is now sending forth a beautiful red vapor; but as we do not want the vapor, Mr. Anderson will hold it near the chimney for a short time, that we may have the use and beauty of the experiment without the annoyance. The copper which I have put into the flask will dissolve: it will change the acid and the water into a blue fluid containing copper and other things, and I propose then showing you how this voltaic battery deals with it. . . .

Now see what happens. These two platinum plates are the two ends of this apparatus; and I am about to put them in contact with that solution. If I put the two platinums in by themselves they come out as clean and as white as they go in; but when we take the power and lay that on, this, you see, is at once turned into copper, as it were; it has become a plate of copper; and that has come out quite clean. If I take this coppered piece and change sides, the copper will leave the right-hand side and come over to the left side; what was before a coppered plate comes out clean, and the plate which was clean comes out coated with copper; and thus you see that the same copper we put into this solution we can also take out of it by means of this instrument.

Putting that solution aside, let us now see what effect this instrument will have upon water. Here are two little platinum plates which I intend to make the ends of the battery, and this (C) is a little vessel so shaped as to enable me to take it to pieces, and show you its construction. In these two cups (A and B) I pour mercury, which touches the ends of the wires connected with the platinum plates. In the vessel (C) I pour some water containing a little acid (but which is put in only for the purpose of facilitating the action; it undergoes no change in the process), and connected with the top of the vessel is a bent glass tube (D), which may remind you of the

pipe which was connected with the gun-barrel in our furnace experiment, and which now passes under the jar (F). I have now adjusted this apparatus, and we will proceed to affect the water in some way or other. In the other case I sent the water through a tube which was made red-hot; I am now going to pass the electricity through the contents of this vessel. Perhaps I may boil the water; if I do boil the water I shall get steam; and you know that steam condenses when it gets cold, and you will therefore see by that whether I do boil the water or not. Perhaps, however, I shall not boil the water, but produce some other effect. You shall have the experiment and see. There is one wire which I will put on this side (A), and here is the other wire which I will put to the other side (B), and you will soon see whether any disturbance takes place. Here it is seeming to boil up famously; but does it boil? Let us see whether that which goes out is steam or not. I think you will soon see the jar (F) will be filled with vapor, if that which rises from the water is steam. But can it be steam? Why, certainly not; because there it remains, you see, unchanged. There it is standing over the water, and it can not therefore be steam, but must be a permanent gas of some sort. What is it? Is it hydrogen? Is it anything else? Well, we will examine it. If it is hydrogen it will burn. It is certainly something combustible, but not combustible in the way that hydrogen is. Hydrogen would not have given you that noise; but the color of that light, when the thing did burn, was like that of hydrogen; it will, however, burn without contact with the air. That is why I have chosen this other form of apparatus, for the purpose of pointing out to you what are the particular circumstances of this experiment. In place of an open vessel, I have taken one that is closed (our battery is so beautifully active that we are even boiling the mercury, and getting all things right—not wrong, but vigorously right); and I am going to show you that that gas, whatever it may be, can burn without air, and in that respect differs from a candle, which can not burn without the air. And our manner of doing

Faraday calculated that to decompose one grain of water as much electricity is required as is contained in a very powerful flash of lightning.

This vessel, having had the air pumped from it, contains a vacuum. When connected to the jar [F] in the previous illustration, the vacuum draws the generated gases into the vessel. These gases are united by an electrical charge to form a small amount of water and a vacuum in the vessel.

A Leyden jar is commonly made with layers of foil lining both the inner and outer surfaces of a jar or bottle. A brass knob projects on a spike through the stopper of the bottle. The jar is used to store charges of static electricity.

this is as follows: I have here a glass vessel (G) which is fitted with two platinum wires (I K) through which I can apply electricity; and we can put the vessel on the air-pump and exhaust the air; and when we have taken the air out we can bring it here and fasten it on to this jar (F), and let into the vessel that gas which was formed by the action of the voltaic battery upon the water, and which we have produced by changing the water into it; for I may go as far as this, and say we have really, by that experiment, changed the water into that gas. We have not only altered its condition, but we have changed it really and truly into that gaseous substance, and all the water is there which was decomposed by the experiment. As I screw this vessel (G H) on here (H), and make the tubes well connected, and when I open the stopcocks (H H H), if you watch the level of the water (in F), you will see that the gas will rise. I will now close the stopcocks, as I have drawn up as much as the vessel can hold, and being safely conveyed into that chamber, I will pass into it an electric spart from this Leyden jar (L), when the vessel, which is now quite clear and bright, will become dim. There will be no sound, for the vessel is strong enough to confine the explosion. Did you see that brilliant light? If I again screw the vessel on to the jar, and open these stopcocks, you will see that the gas will rise a second time. Those gases have disappeared, as you see; their place is vacant, and fresh gas has gone in. Water has been formed from them; and if we repeat our operation, I shall have another vacancy, as you will see by the water rising. I always have an empty vessel after the explosion, because the vapor or gas into which the water has been resolved by the battery explodes under the influence of the spark, and changes into water; and by-and-by you will see in this upper vessel some drops of water trickling down the sides and collecting at the bottom.

We are here dealing with water entirely, without reference to the atmosphere. The water of the candle had the atmosphere helping to produce it; but in this way it can be

produced independently of the air. Water, therefore, ought to contain that other substance which the candle takes from the air, and which, combining with the hydrogen, produces water.

The Other Part of Water

Just now you saw that one end of this battery took hold of the copper, extracting it from the vessel which contained the blue solution. It was effected by this wire; and surely we may say, if the battery has such power with a metallic solution which we made and unmade, may we not find that it is possible to split asunder the component parts of the water, and put them into this place and that place? Suppose I take the poles—the metallic ends of this battery—and see what will happen with the water in this apparatus, where we have separated the two ends far apart. I place one here (at A), and the other there (at B); and I have little shelves with holes which I can put upon each pole, and so arrange them that whatever escapes from the two ends of the battery will appear as separate gases; for you saw that the water did not become vaporous, but gaseous. The wires are now in perfect and proper connection with the vessel containing the water, and you see the bubbles rising; let us collect these bubbles and see what they are. Here is a glass cylinder (O); I fill it with water and put it over one end (A) of the pile, and I will take another (H), and put it over the other end (B) of the pile. And so now we have a double apparatus, with both places delivering gas. Both these jars will fill with gas. There they go, that to the right (H) filling very rapidly; the one to the left (O) filling not so rapidly; and, though I have allowed some bubbles to escape, yet still the action is going on pretty regularly; and were it not that one is rather smaller than the other, you would see that I should have twice as much in this (H) as I have in that (O). Both these gases are colorless; they stand over the water without condensing; they are alike in all things—I mean in all *apparent* things; and we have here an

EXPERIMENT 15, p. 106

The gases given off at the electrodes are collected separately at different rates; oxygen on the left and hydrogen on the right.

opportunity of examining these bodies and ascertaining what they are. Their bulk is large, and we can easily apply experiments to them. I will take this jar (H) first, and will ask you to be prepared to recognize hydrogen.

Think of all its qualities—the light gas which stood well in inverted vessels, burning with a pale flame at the mouth of the jar, and see whether this gas does not satisfy all these conditions. If it be hydrogen it will remain here while I hold this jar inverted. What is there now in the other jar? You know that the two together made an explosive mixture. But what can this be which we find as the other constituent in water, and which must therefore be that substance which made the hydrogen burn? We know that the water we put into the vessel consisted of the two things together. We find one of these is hydrogen: what must the other be which was in the water before the experiment, and which we now have by itself? I am about to put this lighted splinter of wood into the gas. The gas itself will not burn, but it will make the splinter of wood burn. See how it invigorates the combustion of the wood, and how it makes it burn far better than the air would make it burn; and now you see by itself that other substance which is contained in the water, and which, must have been taken from the atmosphere. What shall we call it, A, B, or C? Let us call it O—call it "Oxygen;" it is a very good, distinct-sounding name. This, then, is the oxygen which was present in the water, forming so large a part of it.

Oxygen

We shall now begin to understand more clearly our experiments and researches, because when we have examined these things once or twice we shall soon see why a candle burns in the air. When we have in this way analyzed the water—that is to say, separated or electrolyzed its parts out of it, we get two volumes of hydrogen and one of the body that burns it. And these two are represented to us on the following diagram, with their weights also stated; and we

shall find that the oxygen is a very heavy body by comparison with the hydrogen. It is the other element in water.

	8 Oxygen	Oxygen	88.9
1 Hydrogen		Hydrogen	11.1
	Water 9	Water	100.0

I had better, perhaps, tell you now how we get this oxygen abundantly, having shown you how we can separate it from the water. Oxygen, as you will immediately imagine, exists in the atmosphere; for how should the candle burn to produce water without it? Such a thing would be absolutely impossible, and chemically impossible without oxygen. Can we get it from the air? Well, there are some very complicated and difficult processes by which we can get it from the air; but we have better processes. There is a substance called the black oxide of manganese; it is a very black-looking mineral, but very useful, and when made red-hot it gives out oxygen. Here is an iron bottle which has had some of this substance put into it, and there is a tube fixed to it, and a fire ready made, and Mr. Anderson will put that retort into the fire, for it is made of iron, and can stand the heat. Here is a salt called chlorate of potassa, which is now made in large quantities for bleaching, and chemical and medical uses, and for pyrotechnic and other purposes. I will take some and mix it with some of the oxide of manganese (oxide of copper, or oxide of iron would do as well), and if I put these together in a retort, far less than a red heat is sufficient to evolve this oxygen from the mixture. You will find in this case that we only want sufficient for our experiments; only, as you will see immediately, if I use too small a charge the first portion of the gas will be mixed with the air already in the retort, and I should be obliged to sacrifice the first portion of the gas because it would be so much diluted with air; the first portion

Potassium chlorate, heated with manganese dioxide liberates oxygen. Potassium chloride and manganese dioxide remain.

EXPERIMENT 16, p. 108

must therefore be thrown away. You will find in this case that a common spirit-lamp is quite sufficient for me to get the oxygen, and so we shall have two processes going on for its preparation. See how freely the gas is coming over from that small portion of the mixture. We will examine it and see what are its properties. Now in this way we are producing, as you will observe, a gas just like the one we had in the experiment with the battery, transparent, undissolved by water, and presenting the ordinary visible properties of the atmosphere. (As this first jar contains the air, together with the first portions of the oxygen set free during the preparation, we will carry it out of the way, and be prepared to make our experiments in a regular, dignified manner.) And inasmuch as that power of making wood, wax, or other things burn, was so marked in the oxygen we obtained by means of the voltaic battery from water, we may expect to find the same property here. We will try it. You see there is the combustion of a lighted taper in air, and here is its combustion in this gas. See how brightly and beautifully it burns! You can also see more than this: you will perceive it is a heavy gas, while the hydrogen would go up like a balloon, or even faster than a balloon, when not encumbered with the weight of the envelope. You may easily see that although we obtained from water twice as much in volume of the hydrogen as of oxygen, it does not follow that we have twice as much in weight, because one is heavy and the other a very light gas. We have means of weighing gases or air; but, without stopping to explain that, let me just tell you what their respective weights are. The weight of a pint of hydrogen is three quarters of a grain; the weight of the same quantity of oxygen is nearly twelve grains. This is a very great difference. The weight of a cubic foot of hydrogen is one twelfth of an ounce; and the weight of a cubic foot of oxygen is one ounce and a third. And so on we might come to masses of matter which may be weighed in the balance, and which we can take account of as hundred-weights and as to tons, as you will see almost immediately.

Now, as regards this very property on oxygen supporting combustion, which we may compare to air, I will take a piece of candle to show it you in a rough way—and the result will be rough. There is our candle burning in the air: how will it burn in oxygen? I have here a jar of this gas, and I am about to put it over the candle for you to compare the action of this gas with that of the air. Why, look at it; it looks something like the light you saw at the poles of the voltaic battery. Think how vigorous that action must be. And yet, during all that action, nothing more is produced than what is produced by the burning of the candle in air. We have the same production of water, and the same phenomena exactly, when we use this gas instead of air, as we have when the candle is burnt in air.

EXPERIMENT 15

But now we have got a knowledge of this new substance, we can look at it a little more distinctly, in order to satisfy ourselves that we have got a good general understanding of this part of the product of a candle. It is wonderful how great the supporting powers of this substance are as regards combustion. For instance, here is a lamp which, simple though it be, is the original, I may say, of a great variety of lamps which are constructed for diverse purposes—for light-houses, microscopic illuminations, and other uses; and if it was proposed to make it burn very brightly, you would say, "If a candle burnt better in oxygen, will not a lamp do the same?" Why, it will do. Mr. Anderson will give me a tube coming from our oxygen-reservoir, and I am about to apply it to this flame, which I will previously make burn badly on purpose. There comes the oxygen: what a combustion that makes! But if I shut it off, what becomes of the lamp? It is wonderful how, by means of oxygen, we get combustion accelerated. But it does not affect merely the combustion of hydrogen, or carbon, or the candle, but it exalts all combustions of the common kind. We will take one which relates to iron, for instance, as you have already seen iron burn a little in the atmosphere. Here is a jar of oxygen, and this is a piece of iron wire; but if it were a bar as thick as my wrist, it

EXPERIMENT 16, p. 108
and EXPERIMENT 22,
p. 117

**The iron wire burns
brightly in the jar of
oxygen.**

would burn the same. I first attach a little piece of wood to
the iron; I then set the wood on fire, and let them both down
together into the jar. The wood is now alight, and there it
burns as wood should burn in oxygen; but it will soon com-
municate its combustion to the iron. The iron is now burning
brilliantly, and will continue so for a long time. As long as we
supply oxygen, so long can we carry on the combustion of
the iron, until the latter is consumed.

We will now put that on one side, and take some other
substance; but we must limit our experiments, for we have
not time to spare for all the illustrations you would have a
right to if we had more time. We will take a piece of sulphur:
you know how sulphur burns in the air; well, we put it into
the oxygen, and you will see that whatever can burn in air
can burn with a far greater intensity in oxygen, leading you to
think that perhaps the atmosphere itself owes all its power of
combustion to this gas. The sulphur is now burning very
quietly in the oxygen; but you can not for a moment mistake
the very high and increased action which takes place when it
is so burnt, instead of being burnt merely in common air.

I am now about to show you the combustion of another
substance—phosphorous. I can do it better for you here than
you can do it at home. This is a very combustible substance;
and it if be so combustible in air, what might you expect it
would be in oxygen? I am about to show it to you not in its
fullest intensity, for if I did we should almost blow the ap-
paratus up; I may even now crack the jar, though I do not
want to break things carelessly. You see how it burns in the
air. But what a glorious light it gives out when I introduce it
into oxygen! There you see the solid particles going off which
cause that combustion to be so brilliantly luminous.

Thus far we have tested this power of oxygen, and the high
combustion it produces by means of other substances. We
must now, for a little while longer, look at it as respects the
hydrogen. You know, when we allowed the oxygen and the
hydrogen derived from the water to mix and burn together,

we had a little explosion. You remember also that when I burnt the oxygen and the hydrogen in a jet together, we got very little light, but great heat; I am now about to set fire to oxygen and hydrogen mixed in the proportion in which they occur in water. Here is a vessel containing one volume of oxygen and two volumes of hydrogen. This mixture is exactly of the same nature as the gas we just now obtained from the voltaic battery; it would be far too much to burn at once; I have therefore arranged to blow soap bubbles with it and burn those bubbles, that we may see by a general experiment or two how this oxygen supports the combustion of the hydrogen. First of all we will see whether we can blow a bubble. Well, there goes the gas. Here I have a bubble. I am receiving them on my hand, and you will perhaps think I am acting oddly in this experiment, but it is to show you that we must not always trust to noise and sounds, but rather to real facts. I am afraid to fire a bubble from the end of the pipe, because the explosion would pass up into the jar and blow it to pieces. This oxygen, then, will unite with the hydrogen, as you see by the phenomena, and hear by the sound, with the utmost readiness of action, and all its power are then taken up in its neutralization of the qualities of the hydrogen.

So now I think you will perceive the whole history of water with reference to oxygen and the air from what we have before said. *Why does a piece of potassium decompose water?* Because it finds oxygen in the water. What is set free when I put it in the water, as I am about to do again? It sets free hydrogen, and the hydrogen burns; but the potassium itself combines with oxygen; and this piece of potassium, in taking the water apart—the water, you may say, derived from the combustion of the candle—takes away the oxygen which the candle took from the air and so sets the hydrogen free; and even if I take a piece of ice, and put a piece of potassium upon it, the beautiful affinities by which the oxygen and the hydrogen are related are such that the ice will absolutely set fire to the potassium. I show this to you to-day in order to

enlarge your ideas of these things, and that you may see how greatly results are modified by circumstances. There is the potassium on the ice, producing a sort of volcanic action.

It will be my place when next we meet, having pointed out these anomalous actions, to show you that none of these extra and strange effects are met with by us—that none of these strange and injurious actions take place when we are burning, not merely a candle, but gas in our streets, or fuel in our fireplaces, so long as we confine ourselves within the laws that Nature has made for our guidance.

Lecture V

Oxygen Present in the Air—Nature of the Atmosphere—Its Properties—Other Products from the Candle—Carbonic Acid—Its Properties

Oxygen Present in the Air

We have now seen that we can produce hydrogen and oxygen from the water that we obtained from the candle. Hydrogen, you know, comes from the candle, and oxygen, you believe, comes from the air. But then you have a right to ask me, "How is it that the air and the oxygen do not equally well burn the candle?" If you remember what happened when I put a jar of oxygen over a piece of candle, you recollect there was a very different kind of combustion to that which took place in the air. Now why is this? It is a very important question, and one I shall endeavor to make you understand; it relates most intimately to the nature of the atmosphere, and is most important to us.

We have several tests for oxygen besides the mere burning of bodies; you have seen a candle burnt in oxygen or in the air; you have seen phosphorus burnt in the air or in oxygen, and you have seen iron filings burnt in oxygen. But we have other tests besides these, and I am about to refer to one or two of them for the purpose of carrying your conviction and your experience farther. Here we have a vessel of oxygen. I

The test-gas here is nitrous oxide, or laughing gas. It is a colorless gas which combines with oxygen to form nitrogen dioxide, the reddish gas formed in the earlier reaction between nitric acid and copper. Upon inhalation, nitrous oxide produces insensibility to pain and mild hysteria, and it is used as an anesthetic for short durations. Prolonged inhalation causes death.

will show its presence to you: if I take a little spark and put it into that oxygen, you know by the experience you gained the last time we met what will happen—if I put that spark into the jar, it will tell you whether we have oxygen here or not. Yes! We have proved it by combustion; and now here is another test for oxygen, which is a very curious and useful one. I have here two jars full of gas, with a plate between them to prevent their mixing; I take the plate away, and the gases are creeping one into the other. "What happens?" say you; "they together produce no such combustion as was seen in the case of the candle." But see how the presence of oxygen is told by its association with this other substance. What a beautifully colored gas I have obtained in this way, showing me the presence of the oxygen! In the same way we can try this experiment by mixing common air with this test-gas. Here is a jar containing air—such air as the candle would burn in, and here is a jar or bottle containing the test-gas. I let them come together over water, and you see the result: the contents of the test-bottle are flowing into the jar of air, and you see I obtain exactly the same kind of action as before, and that shows me that there is oxygen in the air—the very same substance that has been already obtained by us from the water produced by the candle. But then, beyond that, how is it that the candle does not burn in air as well as in oxygen? We will come to that point at once. I have here two jars; they are filled to the same height with gas, and the appearance to the eye is alike in both, and I really do not know at present which of these jars contains oxygen and which contains air, although I know they have previously been filled with these gases. But here is our test-gas, and I am going to work with the two jars, in order to examine whether there is any difference between them in the quality of reddening this gas. I am now going to turn this test-gas into one of the jars, and observe what happens: There is reddening, you see; there is, then, oxygen present. We will now test the other jar; but you see this is not so distinctly red

as the first, and farther, this curious thing happens: if I take these two gases and shake them well together with water, we shall absorb the red gas; and then, if I put in more of this test-gas and shake again, we shall absorb more; and I can go on as long as there be any oxygen present to produce that effect. If I let in air, it will not matter; but the moment I introduce water, the red gas disappears; and I may go on in this way, putting in more and more of the test-gas, until I come to something left behind which will not redden any longer by the use of that particular body that rendered the air and the oxygen red. Why is that? You see in a moment it is because there is, besides oxygen, something else present which is left behind. I will let a little more air into the jar, and if it turns red you will know that some of that reddening gas is still present, and that, consequently, it was not for the want of this producing body that that air was left behind.

Now you will begin to understand what I am about to say. You saw that when I burnt phosphorus in a jar, as the smoke produced by the phosphorus and the oxygen of the air condensed, it left a good deal of gas unburnt, just as this red gas left something untouched; there was, in fact, this gas left behind, which the phosphorus can not touch, which the reddening gas can not touch, and this something is not oxygen, and yet is part of the atmosphere.

Nature of the Atmosphere—Its Properties

So that is one way of opening out air into the two things of which it is composed—oxygen, which burns our candles, our phosphorus, or any thing else, and this other substance—nitrogen—which will not burn them. This other part of the air is by far the larger proportion, and it is a curious body. It shows no brilliant effects of combustion. If I test it with a taper as I do oxygen and hydrogen, it does not burn like hydrogen, nor does it make the taper burn like oxygen. Try it any way I will, it does neither the one thing nor the other; it will not take fire; it will not let the taper burn; it puts out the

combustion of everything. There is nothing that will burn in it in common circumstances. It has no smell; it is not sour; it does not dissolve in water; it is neither an acid nor an alkali; it is as indifferent to all our organs as it is possible for a thing to be. And you might say, "It is nothing; it is not worth chemical attention; what does it do in the air?"

Suppose, in place of having nitrogen, or nitrogen oxygen, we had pure oxygen in our atmosphere; what would become of us? You know very well that a piece of iron lit in a jar of oxygen goes on burning to the end. When you see a fire in an iron grate, imagine where the grate would go to if the whole of the atmosphere were oxygen. The grate would burn up more powerfully than the coals; for the iron of the grate itself is even more combustible than the coals which we burn in it. A fire put into the middle of a locomotive would be a fire in a magazine of fuel, if the atmosphere were oxygen. The nitrogen lowers it down and makes it moderate and useful for us, and then, with all that, it takes away with it the fumes that you have seen produced from the candle, disperses them throughout the whole of the atmosphere, and carries them away to places where they are wanted. This nitrogen in its ordinary state is an inactive element; no action short of the most intense electric force, and then in the most infinitely small degree, can cause the nitrogen to combine directly with the other element of the atmosphere, or with other things round about it; it is a perfectly indifferent, and therefore, a safe substance.

But, before I take you to that result, I must tell you about the atmosphere itself. I have written on this diagram the composition of one hundred parts of atmospheric air:

The atmosphere is described by Faraday as 23.3% oxygen and 77.7% nitrogen. As he says, this is a true analysis so far as the quantities of nitrogen and oxygen present— however air also contains small amounts of carbon dioxide and argon as well as traces of neon, helium, krypton, xenon, hydrogen and ozone. These are the elements present in dry air; most air contains some water vapor as well.

	Bulk	Weight
Oxygen	20	23.3
Nitrogen	80	77.7
	100	100.0

It is a true analysis of the atmosphere so far as regards the quantity of oxygen and the quantity of nitrogen present. By our analysis, we find that 5 pints of the atmosphere contain only 1 pint of oxygen, and 4 pints, or 4 parts, of nitrogen by bulk. That is our analysis of the atmosphere. It requires all that quantity of nitrogen to reduce the oxygen down, so as to be able to supply the candle properly with fuel, so as to supply us with an atmosphere which our lungs can healthily and safely breathe; for it is just as important to make the oxygen right for us to breathe, as it is to make the atmosphere right for the burning of the fire and the candle.

But now for this atmosphere. First of all, let me tell you the weight of these gases. A pint of nitrogen weighs 10 4/10 grains, or a cubic foot weighs 1 1/6 ounces. That is the weight of the nitrogen. The oxygen is heavier: a pint of it weighs 11 9/10 grs., and a cubic foot weighs 1 3/4 oz. A pint of air weighs about 10 7/10 grs., and a cubic foot 1 1/5 oz.

You have asked me several times, and I am very glad you have, "How do you weigh gases?" I will show you: it is very simple, and easily done. Here is a balance, and here a copper bottle made as light as we can consistent with due strength, turned very nicely in the lathe, and made perfectly air-tight, with a stopcock, which we can open and shut, which at present is open, and, therefore, allows the bottle to be full of air. I have here a nicely-adjusted balance in which I think the bottle, in its present condition will be balanced by the weight on the other side. And here is a pump by which we can force the air into this bottle, and with it we will force in a certain number of volumes of air as measured by the pump. We will shut that in and put it in the balance. See how it sinks; it is much heavier than it was. By what? By the air that we have forced into it by the pump. There is not a greater *bulk* of air, but there is the same bulk of *heavier* air, because we have forced in air upon it. And that you may have a fair notion in your mind as to how much this air measures, here is a jar full of water. We will open that copper vessel into this jar, and let

Air is forced into a copper bottle using a pump. This bottle is weighed and compared to the normal open-weight of the bottle. The volume of air can be ascertained by determining the amount of water it displaces in an inverted jar.

57

the air return to its former state. All I have to do now is to screw them tightly together, and to turn the taps, when there, you see, is the bulk of twenty pumps of air which I forced into the bottle; and to make sure that we have been quite correct in what we have been doing, we will take the bottle again to the balance, and if it is now counterpoised by the original weight, we shall be quite sure we have made our experiment correctly. It is balanced; so, you see, we can find out the weight of the extra volumes of air forced in in that way, and by that means we are able to ascertain that a cubic foot of air weighs 1 1/5 oz. But that small experiment will by no means convey to your mind the whole literal truth of this matter. It is wonderful how it accumulates when you come to larger volumes. This bulk of air weighs 1 1/5 oz. What do you think of the contents of that box above there which I have had made for the purpose? The air which is within that box weighs one pound—a full pound; and I have calculated the weight of the air in this room: you would hardly imagine it, but it is above a ton. So rapidly do the weights rise up, and so important is the presence of the atmosphere, and of the oxygen and the nitrogen in it, and the use it performs in conveying things to and fro from place to place, and carrying bad vapors to places where they will do good instead of harm.

> To find out the weight of the air in your room, multiply the length x the width x the height. This volume can then be multiplied by 3/40 to get the weight in pounds.
>
> EXPERIMENT 17, p. 109

Having given you that little illustration with respect to the weight of the air, let me show you certain consequences of it. You have a right to them, because you would not understand so much without it. Do you remember this kind of experiment? Have you seen it? Suppose I take a pump somewhat similar to the one I had a little while ago to force air into the bottle, and suppose I place it in such a manner that by certain arrangements I can apply my hand to it. My hand moves about in the air so easily that it seems to feel nothing, and I can hardly get velocity enough by any motion of my own in the atmosphere to make sure that there is much resistance to it. But when I put my hand here you see what happens. Why

is my hand fastened to this place, and why am I able to pull this pump about? And see! how is it that I can hardly get my hand away? Why is this? It is the weight of the air—the weight of the air that is above. I have another experiment here, which I think will explain to you more about it. When the air is pumped from underneath the bladder which is stretched over this glass, you will see the effect in another shape: the top is quite flat at present, but I will make a very little motion with the pump, and now look at it; see how it has gone down; see how it is bent in; you will see the bladder go in more and more, until, at last, I expect it will be driven in and broken by the force of the atmosphere pressing upon it. Now that was done entirely by the weight of the air pressing on it, and you can easily understand how that is. The particles that are piled up in the atmosphere stand upon each other, as these five cubes do; you can easily conceive that four of these five cubes are resting upon the bottom one, and if I take that away the others will all sink down. So it is with the atmosphere; the air that is above is sustained by the air that is beneath, and when the air is pumped away from beneath them, the change occurs which you saw when I placed my hand on the air-pump, and which you saw in the case of the bladder, and which you shall see better here. I have tied over this jar a piece of sheet India-rubber, and I am now about to take away the air from the inside of the jar; and if you will watch the India-rubber—which acts as a partition between the air below and the air above—you will see, when I pump, how the pressure shows itself. See where it is going to: I can actually put my hand into the jar; and yet this result is only caused by the great and powerful action of the air above. How beautifully it shows this curious circumstance!

Here is something that you can have a pull at when I have finished today. It is a little apparatus of two hollow brass hemispheres, closely fitted together, and having connected with it a pipe and a cock, through which we can exhaust the air from the inside; and although the two halves are so easily

This "bladder" is a flexible or stretchable membrane.

The brass sphere is divided but when a vacuum is created inside the two halves are held together tightly by atmospheric pressure.

The toy called a sucker is a round piece of leather with a string through the center When this disc is wetted and laid upon a smooth surface and drawn up by the string, it adheres due to the vacuum created. A game was played with these disks in which the winner was the boy able to use his to pick up the largest stone.

EXPERIMENT 18, p. 111

taken apart while the air is left within, yet you will see, when we exhaust it by-and-by, no power of any two of you will be able to pull them apart. Every square inch of surface that is contained in the area of that vessel sustains fifteen pounds by weight, or nearly so, when the air is taken out, and you may try your strength presently in seeing whether you can overcome that pressure of the atmosphere.

Here is another pretty thing—the boy's sucker, only refined by the philosopher. We young ones have a perfect right to take toys, and make them into philosophy, inasmuch as nowadays we are turning philosophy into toys. Here is a sucker, only it is made of India-rubber. If I clap it upon the table, you see at once it holds. Why does it hold? I can slip it about, and yet if I try to pull it up, it seems as if it would take the table with it. I can easily make it slip about from place to place, but only when I bring it to the edge of the table can I get it off. It is only kept down by the pressure of the atmosphere above; we have a couple of them, and if you take these two and press them together, you will see how firmly they stick. And, indeed, we may use them as they are proposed to be used, to stick against windows or against walls, where they will adhere for an evening, and serve to hang any thing on that you want. I think, however, that you boys ought to be shown experiments that you can make at home; and so here is a very pretty experiment in illustration of the pressure of the atmosphere. Here is a tumbler of water. Suppose I were to ask you to turn that tumbler upside down so that the water should not fall out, and yet not be kept in by your hand, but merely by using the pressure of the atmosphere; could you do that? Take a wine-glass, either quite full or half full of water, and put a flat card on the top; turn it upside down, and then see what becomes of the card and of the water. The air can not get in because the water, by its capillary attraction round the edge, keeps it out.

I think this will give you a correct notion of what you may call the materiality of the air; and when I tell you that that

box holds a pound of it, and this room more than a ton, you will begin to think that air is something very serious. I will make another experiment to convince you of the positive resistance. There is that beautiful experiment of the popgun, made so well and so easily, you know, out of a quill, or a tube, or any thing of that kind; where we take a slice of potato, for instance, or an apple, and take the tube and cut out a pellet, as I have now done, and push it to one end. I have made that end tight; and now I take another piece and put it in: it will confine the air that is within the tube perfectly and completely for our purpose; and I shall now find it absolutely impossible by any force of mine to drive that little pellet close up to the other. It can not be done; I may press the air to a certain extent, but if I go on pressing, long before it comes to the second the confined air will drive the front one out with a force something like that of gunpowder; for gunpowder is in part dependent upon the same action that you see here exemplified.

Faraday's popgun, whereby the force on the pellet at one end compresses the air in the tube until the pellet on the extreme end is forced out with a "pop."

I saw the other day an experiment which pleased me much, as I thought it would serve our purpose here. (I ought to have held my tongue for four or five minutes before beginning this experiment, because it depends upon my lungs for success.) By the proper application of air, I expect to be able to drive this egg out of one cup into the other by the force of my breath; but if I fail it is in a good cause, and I do not promise success, because I have been talking more than I ought to do to make the experiment succeed.

You see that the air which I blow goes downward between the egg and the cup, and makes a blast under the egg, and is thus able to lift a heavy thing; for a full egg is a very heavy thing for air to lift. If you want to make the experiment, you had better boil the egg quite hard first, and then you may very safely try to blow it from one cup to the other with a little care.

Blowing hard and suddenly between the egg and the cup momentarily compresses the air between them, causing the egg to jump out.

I have now kept you long enough upon this property of the weight of the air, but there is another thing I should like to

When a vacuum is created in a jar which has an inflated balloon inside, the air in the balloon expands to fill the jar.

mention. You saw the way in which, in this popgun, I was able to drive the second piece of potato half or two thirds of an inch before the first piece started, by virtue of the elasticity of the air, just as I pressed into the copper bottles the particles of air by means of the pump. Now this depends upon a wonderful property in the air, namely, its elasticity, and I should like to give you a good illustration of this. If I take any thing that confines the air properly, as this membrane, which also is able to contract and expand so as to give us a measure of the elasticity of the air, and confine in this bladder a certain portion of air; and then, if we take the atmosphere off from the outside of it, just as in these cases we put the pressure on—if we take the pressure off, you will see how it will then go on expanding and expanding, larger and larger, until it will fill the whole of this bell-jar, showing you that wonderful property of the air, its elasticity, its compressibility, and expansibility, to an exceedingly large extent, and which is very essential for the purposes and services it performs in the economy of creation.

Other Products from the Candle

We will now turn to another very important part of our subject, remembering that we have examined the candle in its burning, and have found that it gives rise to various products. We have the products, you know, of soot, of water, and of something else, which you have not yet examined. We have collected the water, but have allowed the other things to go into the air. Let us now examine some of these other products.

Here is an experiment which I think will help you in part in this way. We will put our candle there, and place over it a chimney, thus. I think my candle will go on burning, because the air-passage is open at the bottom and the top. In the first place, you see the moisture appearing—that you know about. It is water produced from the candle by the action of the air upon its hydrogen. But, besides that, something is

going out at the top: it is not moisture—it is not water—it is not condensible; and yet, after all, it has very singular properties. You will find that the air coming out of the top of our chimney is nearly sufficient to blow the light out I am holding to it; and if I put the light fairly opposed to the current, it will blow it quite out. You will say, that is as it should be, and I am supposing that you think it ought to do so, because the nitrogen does not support combustion, and ought to put the candle out, since the candle will not burn in nitrogen. But is there nothing else there than nitrogen? I must now anticipate—that is to say, I must use my own knowledge to supply you with the means that we adopt for the purpose of ascertaining these things, and examining such gases as these. I will take an empty bottle—here is one—and if I hold it over this chimney, I shall get the combustion of the candle below sending its results into the bottle above; and we shall soon find that this bottle contains not merely an air that is bad as regards the combustion of a taper put into it, but having other properties.

The air proceeding from the chimney is not sufficient to "blow out" a flame—yet the air will not support combustion.

Let me take a little quick-lime and pour some common water on to it—the commonest water will do. I will stir it a moment, then pour it upon a piece of filtering paper in a funnel, and we shall very quickly have a clear water proceeding to the bottle below, as I have here. I have plenty of this water in another bottle, but nevertheless I should like to use the lime-water that was prepared before you, so that you may see what its uses are. If I take some of this beautiful clear lime-water, and pour it into this jar which has collected the air from the candle, you will see a change coming about. Do you see that the water has become quite milky? Observe, that will not happen with air merely. Here is a bottle filled with air; and if I put a little lime-water into it, neither the oxygen nor the nitrogen, nor anything else that is in that quantity of air, will make any change in the lime-water; it remains perfectly clear, and no shaking of that quantity of lime-water with that quantity of air in its common state will

Calcium hydroxide (slaked lime) is used to make limewater.

EXPERIMENT 19, p. 113

63

cause any change; but if I take this bottle with the lime-water and hold it so as to get the general products of the candle in contact with it, in a very short time we shall have it milky; there is the chalk, consisting of the lime which we used in making the lime-water, combined with something that came from the candle—that other product which we are in search of, and which I want to tell you about today. This is a substance made visible to us by its action, which is not the action of the lime-water either upon the oxygen or upon the nitrogen, nor upon the water itself, but it is something new to us from the candle. And then we find this white powder, produced by the lime-water and the vapor from the candle, appears to us very much like whitening or chalk, and when examined it does prove to be exactly the same substance as whitening or chalk. So we are led, or have been led, to observe upon the various circumstances of this experiment, and to trace this production of chalk to its various causes, to give us the true knowledge of the nature of this combustion of the candle—to find that this substance issuing from the candle is exactly the same as that substance which would issue from a retort if I were to put some chalk into it with a little moisture and make it red-hot; you would then find that exactly the same substance would issue from it as from the candle.

Carbonic Acid

Joseph Black (1728-1799) was a chemist best known for his "rediscovery" of "fixed air" or carbon dioxide. Carbon dioxide had previously been described by Jan van Helmont (1577-1644) as "gas sylvestre."

Black showed that carbon dioxide is produced by fermentation, respiration and the burning of charcoal.

But we have a better means of getting this substance, and in greater quantity, so as to ascertain what its general characters are. We find this substance in very great abundance in a multitude of cases where you would least expect it. All limestones contain a great deal of this gas which issues from the candle, and which we call *carbonic acid*. All chalks, all shells, all corals, contain a great quantity of this curious air. We find it fixed in these stones, for which reason Dr. Black called it "fixed air"—finding it in these fixed things like marble and chalk—he called it fixed air because it lost its

quality of air, and assumed the condition of a solid body. We can easily get this air from marble. Here is a jar containing a little muriatic acid, and here is a taper which, if I put it into the jar, will show only the presence of common air. There is, you see, pure air down to the bottom; the jar is full of it. Here is a substance—marble—a very beautiful and superior marble; and if I put these pieces of marble into the jar, a great boiling apparently goes on. That, however, is not steam; it is a gas that is rising up; and if I now search the jar by a candle, I shall have exactly the same effect produced upon the taper as I had from the air which issued from the end of the chimney over the burning candle. It is exactly the same action, and caused by the very same substance that issued from the candle; and in this way we can get carbonic acid in great abundance—we have already nearly filled the jar. We also find that this gas is not merely contained in marble. Here is a vessel in which I have put some common whitening—chalk which has been washed in water and deprived of its coarser particles, and so supplied to the plasterer as whitening—here is a large jar containing this whitening and water; and I have here some strong sulphuric acid, which is the acid you might have to use if you were to make these experiments (only, in using this acid with limestone, the body that is produced is an insoluble substance, whereas the muriatic acid produces a soluble substance that does not so much thicken the water). And you will seek out a reason why I take this kind of apparatus for the purpose of showing this experiment. I do it because you may repeat in a small way what I am about to do in a large one. You will have here just the same kind of action; and I am evolving in this large jar carbonic acid exactly the same in its nature and properties as the gas which we obtained from the combustion of the candle in the atmosphere. And, no matter how different the two methods by which we prepare this carbonic acid, you will see, when we get to the end of our subject, that it is all exactly the same, whether prepared in one way or the other.

Muriatic acid (HCl) is hydrochloric acid. (The acid was formerly thought to be an oxide of a theorized element—murium—and muriatic acid was its accepted scientific name.)

Marble is a compound of carbonic acid and lime. The muriatic acid, being the stronger of the two acids, takes the place of the carbonic acid, which escapes as a gas, the residue forming muriate of lime or chloride of calcium.
EXPERIMENT 20, p. 114

Carbonic acid is an acid, H_2CO_2, which exists only in solution. It breaks up readily into water and carbon dioxide, CO_2, which is hence commonly called carbonic acid gas or, sometimes, simply, carbonic acid.

We will now proceed to the next experiment with regard to this gas. What is its nature? Here is one of the vessels full, and we will try it as we have done so many other gases—by combustion. You see it is not combustible, nor does it support combustion. Neither, as we know, does it dissolve much in water, because we collect it over water very easily. Then you know that it has an effect, and becomes white in contact with lime-water; and when it does become white in that way, it becomes one of the constituents to make carbonate of lime or limestone.

The next thing I must show you is that it really does dissolve a little in water, and therefore that it is unlike oxygen and hydrogen in that respect. In the lower part of this apparatus is marble and acid, and in the upper part cold water. The valves are so arranged that the gas can get from one to the other. I will set it in action now, and you can see the gas bubbling up through the water, as it has been doing all night long, and by this time we shall find that we have this substance dissolved in the water. It is impregnated with the carbonic acid; and if I apply a little lime-water to it, that will give us a test of its presence. This water will make the lime-water turbid and white, which is proof of the presence of carbonic acid.

Then it is a very weighty gas; it is heavier than the atmosphere. I have put their respective weights at the lower part of this table, along with, for comparison, the weights of the other gases we have been examining:

Gas	per pint
Hydrogen	.75 grs.
Oxygen	11.90
Nitrogen	10.40
Air	10.70
Carbonic acid	16.33

A pint of it weighs 16.33 grs., and a cubic foot weighs 1.9 oz., almost two ounces. You can see by many experiments

that this is a heavy gas. Suppose I take a glass containing nothing else but air, and from this vessel containing the carbonic acid I attempt to pour a little of this gas into that glass—I wonder whether any has gone in or not. I can not tell by the appearance, but I can in this way. Yes, there it is, you see; and if I were to examine it by lime-water, I should find it by that test also. I will take this little bucket, and put it down into the well of carbonic acid—indeed, we too often have real wells of carbonic acid—and now, if there is any carbonic acid, I must have got to it by this time, and it will be in this bucket, which we will examine with a taper. There it is, you see: it is full of carbonic acid.

There is another experiment by which I will show you its weight. I have here a jar suspended at one end of a balance—it is now equipoised; but when I put this carbonic acid into the jar on the one side which now contains air, you will see it sink down at once because of the carbonic acid that I pour into it. And now, if I examine this jar with the lighted taper, I shall find that the carbonic acid has fallen into it, and it no longer has any power of supporting the combustion. If I blow a soap-bubble, which of course will be filled with air and let it fall into this jar of carbonic acid it will float. But I shall first of all take one of these little balloons filled with air. I am not quite sure where the carbonic acid is; we will just try the depth, and see whereabouts is its level. There, you see, we have this bladder floating on the carbonic acid; and if I evolve some more of the carbonic acid, the bladder will be lifted up higher. There it goes; the jar is nearly full, and now I will see whether I can blow a soap-bubble on that and float it in the same way. It is floating as the balloon floated by virtue of the greater weight of the carbonic acid than of the air. And now, having so far given you the history of the carbonic acid, as to its sources in the candle, as to its physical properties and weight, when we next meet I shall show you of what it is composed, and where it gets its elements from.

EXPERIMENT 21, p. 116

Carbon dioxide is heavier than air and is contained by the jar. The bubble of air floats in the carbon dioxide as if it were an ice cube in water.

Lecture VI

Carbon or Charcoal—Coal-gas—Respiration and its Analogy to the Burning of a Candle—Conclusion

Carbon or Charcoal

I told you, when we last met, a good deal about carbonic acid. We found by the lime-water test that when the vapor from the top of the candle or lamp was received into bottles and tested by this solution of lime-water (the composition of which I explained to you, and which you can make for yourselves), we had that white opacity which was in fact calcareous matter, like shells and corals, and many of the rocks and minerals in the earth. But I have not yet told you fully and clearly the chemical history of this substance, carbonic acid, as we have it from the candle, and I must now resume that subject. We have seen the products, and the nature of them, as they issue from the candle. We have traced the water to its elements, and now we have to see where are the elements of the carbonic acid supplied by the candle: a few experiments will show this. You remember that when a candle burns badly it produces smoke; but if it is burning well, there is no smoke. And you know that the brightness of the candle is due to this smoke, which becomes ignited. Here is an experiment to prove this: so long as the smoke remains

The adjective calcareous denotes any substance consisting of or containing, calcium.

in the flame of the candle and becomes ignited, it gives a beautiful light, and never appears to us in the form of black particles. I will light some fuel which is extravagant in its burning: this will serve our purpose—a little turpentine on a sponge. You see the smoke rising from it, and floating into the air in large quantities; and remember now, the carbonic acid that we have from the candle is from such smoke as that. To make that evident to you, I will introduce this turpentine burning on the sponge into a flask where I have plenty of oxygen, the rich part of the atmosphere, and you now see that the smoke is all consumed. This is the first part of our experiment; and now what follows? The carbon which you saw flying off from the turpentine flame in the air is now entirely burned in this oxygen, and we shall find that it will, by this rough and temporary experiment, give us exactly the same conclusion and result as we had from the combustion of the candle. The reason why I make the experiment in this manner is solely that I may cause the steps of our demonstration to be so simple that you can never for a moment lose the train of reasoning, if you only pay attention. All the carbon which is burned in oxygen, or air, comes out as carbonic acid, while those particles which are not so burned show you the second substance in the carbonic acid, namely, the carbon—that body which made the flame so bright while there was plenty of air, but which was thrown off in excess when there was not oxygen enough to burn it.

EXPERIMENT 22, p. 117

I have also to show you a little more distinctly the history of carbon and oxygen in their union to make carbonic acid. You are now better able to understand this than before, and I have prepared three or four experiments by way of illustration. This jar is filled with oxygen, and here is some carbon which has been placed in a crucible for the purpose of being made red-hot. I am about to put the oxygen and carbon together. That this is carbon (common charcoal pulverized) you will see by the way in which it burns in the air [letting some of the red-hot charcoal fall out of the crucible]. I am

EXPERIMENT 22, p. 117

now about to burn it in oxygen gas, and look at the difference. It may appear to you at a distance as if it were burning with a flame: but it is not so. Every little piece of charcoal is burning as a spark, and while it so burns it is producing carbonic acid. I specially want these two or three experiments to point out what I shall dwell upon more distinctly by-and-by—that carbon burns in this way, and not as a flame.

Instead of taking many particles of carbon to burn I will take a rather large piece, which will enable you to see the form and size, and to trace the effects very decidedly. Here is the jar of oxygen, and here is the piece of charcoal, to which I have fastened a little piece of wood, which I can set fire to, and so commence the combustion, which I could not conveniently do without. You now see the charcoal burning, but not as a flame (or if there be a flame it is the smallest possible one, which I know the cause of, namely, the formation of a little carbonic oxide close upon the surface of the carbon). It goes on burning, you see, slowly producing carbonic acid by the union of this carbon or charcoal (they are equivalent terms) with the oxygen. I have here another piece of charcoal, a piece of bark, which has the quality of being blown to pieces—exploding—as it burns. By the effect of the heat we shall reduce the lump of carbon into particles that will fly off; still every particle, equally with the whole mass, burns in this peculiar way—it burns as a coal and not like a flame. You observe a multitude of little combustions going on, but no flame. I do not know a finer experiment than this to show that carbon burns with a spark.

Here, then, is carbonic acid formed from its elements. It is produced at once; and if we examined it by lime-water you will see that we have the same substance which I have previously described to you. By putting together 6 parts of carbon by weight (whether it comes from the flame of a candle or from powdered charcoal) and 16 parts of oxygen by weight, we have 22 parts of carbonic acid; and, as we saw

70

last time, the 22 parts of carbonic acid combined with 28 parts of lime, produced common carbonate of lime. If you were to examine an oyster-shell and weigh the component parts, you would find that every 50 parts would give 6 of carbon and 16 of oxygen combined with 28 of lime. However, I do not want to trouble you with these minutiae; it is only the general philosophy of the matter that we can now go into. See how finely the carbon is dissolving away [pointing to the lump of charcoal burning in the jar of oxygen]. You may say that the charcoal is actually dissolving in the air round about; and if that were perfectly pure charcoal, which we can easily prepare, there would be no residue whatever. When we have a perfectly cleansed and purified peace of carbon, there is no ash left. The carbon burns as a solid dense body, that heat alone can not change as to its solidity, and yet it passes away into vapor that never condenses into solid or liquid under ordinary circumstances; and what is more curious still is the fact that the oxygen does not change in its bulk by the solution of the carbon in it. Just as the bulk is at first, so it is at last, only it has become carbonic acid.

There is another experiment which I must give you before you are fully acquainted with the general nature of carbonic acid. Being a compound body, consisting of carbon and oxygen, carbonic acid is a body that we ought to be able to take asunder. And so we can. As we did with water, so we can with carbonic acid—take the two parts asunder. The simplest and quickest way is to act upon the carbonic acid by a substance that can attract the oxygen from it, and leave the carbon behind. You recollect that I took potassium and put it upon water or ice, and you saw that it could take the oxygen from the hydrogen. Now, suppose we do something of the same kind here with this carbonic acid. You know carbonic acid to be a heavy gas: I will not test it with lime-water, as that will interfere with our subsequent experiments, but I think the heaviness of the gas and the power of extinguishing

flame will be sufficient for our purpose. I introduce a flame into the gas, and you will see whether it will be put out. You see the light is extinguished. Indeed, the gas may, perhaps, put out phosphorus, which you know has a pretty strong combustion. Here is a piece of phosphorus heated to a high degree. I introduce it into gas, and you observe the light is put out, but it will take fire again in the air, because there it re-enters into combustion. Now let me take a piece of potassium, a substance which even at common temperatures can act upon carbonic acid, though not sufficiently for our present purpose, because it soon gets covered with a protecting coat; but if we warm it up to the burning point in air, as we have a fair right to do, and as we have done with phosphorus, you will see that it can burn in carbonic acid; and if it burns, it will burn by taking oxygen, so that you will see what is left behind. I am going, then, to burn this potassium in the carbonic acid, as a proof of the existence of oxygen in the carbonic acid. [As Faraday was heating the potassium it exploded.] Sometimes we get an awkward piece of potassium that explodes, or something like it, when it burns. I will take another piece, and now that it is heated I introduce it into the jar, and you perceive that it burns in the carbonic acid— not so well as in the air, because the carbonic acid contains the oxygen combined; but it does burn, and takes away the oxygen. If I now put this potassium into water, I find that besides the potash formed (which you need not trouble about) there is a quantity of carbon produced. I have here made the experiment in a very rough way, but I assure you that if I were to make it carefully, devoting a day to it instead of five minutes, we should get all the proper amount of charcoal left in the spoon, or in the place where the potassium was burned, so that there could be no doubt as to the result. Here, then, is the carbon obtained from the carbonic acid, as a common black substance; so that you have the entire proof of the nature of carbonic acid as consisting of carbon and oxygen. And now I may tell you, that

whenever carbon burns under common circumstances it produces carbonic acid.

Suppose I take this piece of wood, and put it into a bottle with lime-water. I might shake that lime-water up with wood and the atmosphere as long as I pleased, it would still remain clear as you see it; but suppose I burn the piece of wood in the air of that bottle. You, of course, know I get water. Do I get carbonic acid? There it is, you see—that is to say, the carbonate of lime, which results from carbonic acid, and that carbonic acid must be formed from the carbon which comes from the wood, from the candle, or any other thing. Indeed, you have yourselves frequently tried a very pretty experiment, by which you may see the carbon in wood. If you take a piece of wood, and partly burn it, and then blow it out, you have carbon left. There are things that do not show carbon in this way. A candle does not so show it, but it contains carbon. Here also is a jar of coal-gas, which produces carbonic acid abundantly; you do not see the carbon, but we can soon show it to you. I will light it, and as long as there is any gas in the cylinder it will go on burning. You see no carbon, but you see a flame, and because that is bright it will lead you to guess that there is carbon in that flame. But I will show it to you by another process. I have some of the same gas in another vessel, mixed with a body that will burn the hydrogen of the gas, but will not burn the carbon. I will light them with a burning taper, and you perceive the hydrogen is consumed, but not the carbon, which is left behind as a dense black smoke. I hope that by these three or four experiments you will learn to see when carbon is present, and understand what are the products of combustion when gas or other bodies are thoroughly burned in the air.

Partly burned wood, showing carbon.

Coal-gas

Before we leave the subject of carbon, let us make a few experiments and remarks upon its wonderful condition as respects ordinary combustion. I have shown you that the

73

carbon, in burning, burns only as a solid body, and yet you perceive that, after it is burned, it ceases to be a solid. There are very few fuels that act like this. It is, in fact, only that great source of fuel, the carbonaceous series, the coals, charcoals, and woods, that can do it. I do not know that there is any other elementary substance besides carbon that burns with these conditions; and if it had not been so, what would happen to us? Suppose all fuel had been like iron, which, when it burns, burns into a solid substance. We could not then have such a combustion as you have in this fireplace. Here also is another kind of fuel which burns very well—as well as, if not better, than carbon—so well, indeed, as to take fire of itself when it is in the air, as you see. [Breaks open a tube full of lead pyrophorus.] This substance is lead, and you see how wonderfully combustible it is. It is very much divided, and is like a heap of coals in the fireplace: the air can get to its surface and inside, and so it burns. But why does it not burn in that way now when it is lying in a mass? [Empties the contents of the tube in a heap on to a plate of iron.] Simply because the air can not get to it. Though it can produce a great heat, the great heat which we want in our furnaces and under our boilers, still that which is produced can not get away from the portion which remains unburned underneath, and that portion, therefore, is prevented from coming in contact with the atmosphere, and can not be consumed. How different is that from carbon! Carbon burns just in the same way as this lead does, and so gives an intense fire in the furnace, or wherever you choose to burn it; but then the body produced by its combustion passes away, and the remaining carbon is left clear. I showed you how carbon went on dissolving in the oxygen, leaving no ash, whereas here we have actually more ash than fuel, for it is heavier by the amount of oxygen which has united with it. Thus you see the difference between carbon and lead or iron—if we choose iron, which gives so wonderful a result in our applications of this fuel, either as light or heat. If, when the carbon

Lead pyrophorus is made by heating dry tartrate of lead in a glass tube (closed at one end, and drawn out to a fine point at the other) until no more vapors are evolved. The open end of the tube is then sealed before the blowpipe. When the tube is broken and the contents shaken out into the air, they burn with a red flash.

burnt, the product went off as a solid body, you would have had the room filled with an opaque substance, as in the case of the phosphorus; but when carbon burns, every thing passes up into the atmosphere. It is in a fixed, almost unchangeable condition before the combustion; but afterward it is in the form of gas, which it is very difficult (though we have succeeded) to produce in a solid or liquid state.

Respiration and Its Analogy to the Burning of a Candle

Now I must take you to a very interesting part of our subject—to the relation between the combustion of a candle and that living kind of combustion which goes on within us. In every one of us there is a living process of combustion going on very similar to that of a candle, and I must try to make that plain to you. For it is not merely true in a poetical sense—the relation of the life of man to a taper; and if you will follow, I think I can make this clear. In order to make the relation very plain, I have devised a little apparatus which we can soon build up before you. Here is a board, and a groove cut in it, and I can close the groove at the top part by a little cover; I can then continue the groove as a channel by a glass tube at each end, there being a free passage through the whole. Suppose I take a taper or candle (we can now be liberal in our use of the word "candle," since we understand what it means), and place it in one of the tubes; it will go on, you see, burning very well. You observe that the air which feeds the flame passes down the tube at one end, then goes along the horizontal tube, and ascends the tube at the other end in which the taper is placed. If I stop the aperture through which the air enters, I stop combustion, as you perceive. I stop the supply of air, and consequently the candle goes out. But now what will you think of this fact? In a former experiment I showed you the air going from one burning candle to a second candle. If I took the air proceeding from another candle, and sent it down by a complicated arrangement into this tube, I should put this burning

Expired air will put out
the candle.

The contents of the
open bell jar support
combustion. When
placed in water, the
entire contents of air in
the jar can be inhaled
and then returned to the
jar. The air in the jar
then contains enough
carbon dioxide to ex-
tinguish the flame.

candle out. But what will you say when I tell you that my breath will put out the candle? I do not mean by blowing at all, but simply that the nature of my breath is such that a candle can not burn in it. I will now hold my mouth over the aperture, and without blowing the flame in any way, let no air enter the tube but what comes from my mouth. You see the result. I did not blow the candle out. I merely let the air which I expired pass into the aperture, and the result was that the light went out for want of oxygen, and for no other reason. Something or other—namely, my lungs—had taken away the oxygen from the air and there was no more to supply the combustion of the candle. It is, I think, very pretty to see the time it takes before the bad air which I throw into this part of the apparatus has reached the candle. The candle at first goes on burning, but so soon as the air has had time to reach it it goes out. And now I will show you another experiment.

Here is a jar which contains fresh air, as you can see by the circumstance of a candle or gaslight burning it. I make it close for a little time, and by means of a pipe I get my mouth over it so that I can inhale the air. By putting it over water, in the way that you see, I am able to draw up this air (supposing the cork to be quite tight), take it into my lungs, and throw it back into the jar: we can then examine it, and see the result. You observe, I first take up the air, and then throw it back, as is evident from the ascent and descent of the water; and now, by putting a taper into the air, you will see that state in which it is by the light being extinguished. Even one inspiration, you see, has completely spoiled this air, so that it is no use my trying to breathe it a second time. Now you understand the ground of the impropriety of many of the arrangements among the houses of the poorer classes, by which the air is breathed over and over again for the want of a supply, by means of proper ventilation, sufficient to produce a good result. You see how bad the air becomes by a single breathing, so that you can easily understand how

essential fresh air is to us.

To pursue this a little farther, let us see what will happen with lime-water. Here is a globe which contains a little lime-water, and it is so arranged as regards the pipes as to give access to the air within, so that we can ascertain the effect of respired or unrespired air upon it. Of course I can either draw in air (through A), and so make the air that feeds my lungs go through the lime-water, or I can force the air out of my lungs through the tube (B), which goes to the bottom, and so show its effect upon the lime-water. You will observe that however long I draw the external air into the lime-water and then through it to my lungs, I shall produce no effect upon the water—it will not make the lime-water turbid; but if I throw the air *from* my lungs through the lime-water several times in succession, you see how white and milky the water is getting, showing the effect which expired air has had upon it; and now you begin to know that the atmosphere which we have spoiled by respiration is spoiled by carbonic acid, for you see it here in contact with the lime-water.

I have here two bottles, both containing lime-water as clear as common water, and tubes which pass into the bottles and connect them. The apparatus is very rough, but it is useful notwithstanding. If I take these two bottles, inhaling here and exhaling there, the arrangement of the tubes will prevent the air going backward. The air coming in will go to my mouth and lungs, and in going out will pass through the lime-water, so that I can go on breathing, and making an experiment very refined in its nature and very good in its results. You will observe that the good air has done nothing to the lime-water; in the other case, nothing has come to the lime-water but my respiration, and you see the difference in the two cases.

Let us now go a little farther. What is all this process going on within us which we cannot do without, either day or night? When we are asleep the organs of respiration and the parts that are associated with them still go on

Sucking in through tube A bubbles atmospheric air from tube B through the limewater which remains clear. Blowing exhaled air through tube B turns limewater milky.

EXPERIMENT 19, p. 113

with their action, so necessary is this process of respiration to us, this contact of the air with the lungs. I must tell you, in the briefest possible manner, what this process is. We consume food; the food goes through that strange set of vessels and organs within us, and is brought into various parts of the system, into the digestive parts especially; and alternately the portion which is so changed is carried through our lungs by one set of vessels, while the air we inhale and exhale is drawn into and thrown out of the lungs by another set of vessels, so that the air and the food come close together, separated only by an exceedingly thin surface: the air can thus act upon the blood by this process, producing precisely the same results in kind as we have seen in the case of the candle. The candle combines with parts of the air forming carbonic acid, and evolves heat; so in the lungs there is this curious, wonderful change taking place. The air entering, combines with the carbon (not carbon in a free state, but, as in this case, placed ready for action at the moment), and makes carbonic acid and is so thrown out into the atmosphere, and thus this singular result takes place; we may thus look upon the food as fuel. Let me take that piece of sugar, which will serve my purpose. It is a compound of carbon, hydrogen, and oxygen, similar to a candle, as containing the same elements, though not in the same proportion, the proportions being as shown in this table:

SUGAR

Carbon	72
Hydrogen	11
Oxygen	88

This is, indeed, a very curious thing, which you can well remember, for the oxygen and hydrogen are in exactly the proportions which form water, so that sugar may be said to be compounded of 72 parts of carbon and 99 parts of water; and it is the carbon in the sugar that combines with the oxygen carried in by the air in the process of respiration, so

making us like candles; producing these actions, warmth, and far more wonderful results besides, for the sustenance of the system, by a most beautiful and simple process. To make this still more striking, I will take a little sugar; or, to hasten the experiment, I will use some syrup, which contains about three fourths of sugar and a little water. If I put a little oil of vitriol on it, it takes away the water, and leaves the carbon in a black mass. You see how the carbon is coming out, and before long we shall have a solid mass of charcoal, all of which has come out of sugar. Sugar, as you know, is food, and here we have absolutely a solid lump of carbon where you would not have expected it. And if I make arrangements so as to oxidize the carbon of sugar we shall have a much more striking result. Here is sugar, and I have here an oxidizer—a quicker one than the atmosphere; and so we shall oxidize this fuel by a process different from respiration in its form, though not different in its kind. It is the combustion of the carbon by the contact of oxygen which the body has supplied to it. If I set this into action at once, you will see combustion produced. Just what occurs in my lungs—taking in oxygen from another source, namely, the atmosphere, takes place here by a more rapid process.

Oil of vitriol was another name for sulphuric acid.

Conclusion

You will be astonished when I tell you what this curious play of carbon amounts to. A candle will burn some four, five, six, or seven hours. What, then, must be the daily amount of carbon going up into the air in the way of carbonic acid! What a quantity of carbon must go from each of us in respiration! What a wonderful change of carbon must take place under these circumstances of combustion or respiration! A man in twenty-four hours converts as much as seven ounces of carbon into carbonic acid; a milch cow will convert seventy ounces, and a horse seventy-nine ounces, solely by the act of respiration. That is, the horse in twenty-four hours burns seventy-nine ounces of charcoal, or carbon,

79

in his organs of respiration to supply his natural warmth in that time. All the warm-blooded animals get their warmth in this way, by the conversion of carbon, not in a free state, but in a state of combination. And what an extraordinary notion this gives us of the alterations going on in our atmosphere. As much as 5,000,000 pounds, or 548 tons, of carbonic acid is formed by respiration in London alone in twenty-four hours. And where does all this go? Up into the air. If the carbon had been like the lead which I showed you, or the iron which, in burning, produces a solid substance, what would happen? Combustion could not go on. As charcoal burns it becomes a vapor and passes off into the atmosphere, which is the great vehicle, the great carrier for conveying it away to other places. Then what becomes of it? Wonderful it is to find that the change produced by respiration, which seems so injurious to us (for we can not breathe air twice over), is the very life and support of plants and vegetables that grow upon the surface of the earth. It is the same also under the surface, in the great bodies of water; for fishes and other animals respire upon the same principle, though not exactly by contact with the open air.

Such fish as I have here [goldfish] respire by the oxygen which is dissolved from the air by the water, and form carbonic acid, and they all move about to produce the one great work of making the animal and vegetable kingdoms subservient to each other. And all the plants growing upon the surface of the earth, like that which I have brought here to serve as an illustration, absorb carbon; these leaves are taking up their carbon from the atmosphere to which we have given it in the form of carbonic acid, and they are growing and prospering. Give them a pure air like ours, and they could not live in it; give them carbon with other matters, and they live and rejoice. This piece of wood gets all its carbon, as the trees and plants get theirs, from the atmosphere, which, as we have seen, carries away what is bad for us and at the same time good for them—what is

disease to the one being health to the other. So are we made dependent not merely upon our fellow-creatures, but upon our fellow-existers, all Nature being tied together by the laws that make one part conduce to the good of another.

There is another little point which I must mention before we draw to a close—a point which concerns the whole of these operations, and most curious and beautiful it is to see it clustering upon and associated with the bodies that concern us—oxygen, hydrogen, and carbon, in different states of their existence. I showed you just now some powdered lead, which I set burning; and you saw that the moment the fuel was brought to the air it acted, even before it got out of the bottle—the moment the air crept in it acted. Now there is a case of chemical affinity by which all our operations proceed. When we breathe, the same operation is going on within us. When we burn a candle, the attraction of the different parts one to the other is going on. Here it is going on in this case of the lead, and it is a beautiful instance of chemical affinity. If the products of combustion rose off from the surface, the lead would take fire, and go on burning to the end; but you remember that we have this difference between charcoal and lead—that, while the lead can start into action at once if there be access of air to it, the carbon will remain days, weeks, months, or years. The manuscripts of Herculaneum were written in carbonaceous ink, and there they have been for 1800 years or more, not having been at all changed under the atmosphere, though coming in contact with it under various circumstances. Now, what is the circumstance which makes the lead and carbon differ in this respect? It is a striking thing to see that the matter which is appointed to serve the purpose of fuel *waits* in its action; it does not start off burning, like the lead and many other things that I could show you, but which I have not encumbered the table with; but it waits for action. This waiting is a curious and wonderful thing. Candles—those Japanese candles, for instance—do not start into action at once like

the lead or iron (for iron finely divided does the same thing as lead), but there they wait for years, perhaps for ages, without undergoing any alteration. I have here a supply of coal-gas. The jet is giving forth the gas, but you see it does not take fire—it comes out into the air, but it waits till it is hot enough before it burns. If I make it hot enough, it takes fire. If I blow it out, the gas that is issuing forth waits till the light is applied to it again. It is curious to see how different substances wait—how some will wait till the temperature is raised a little, and others till it is raised a good deal. I have here a little gunpowder and some gun-cotton; even these things differ in the conditions under which they will burn. The gunpowder is composed of carbon and other substances, making it highly combustible; and the gun-cotton is another combustible preparation. They are both waiting, but they will start into activity at different degrees of heat, or under different conditions. By applying a heated wire to them, we shall see which will start first [puts heated wire to the gun-cotton]. You see the gun-cotton has gone off, but not even the hottest part of the wire is now hot enough to fire the gun-powder. How beautifully that shows you the difference in the degree in which bodies act in this way! In the one case the substance will wait any time until the associated bodies are made active by heat; but in the other, as in the process of respiration, it waits no time. In the lungs, as soon as the air enters, it unites with the carbon; even in the lowest temperature which the body can bear short of being frozen, the action begins at once, producing the carbonic acid of respiration; and so all things go on fitly and properly. Thus you see the analogy between respiration and combustion is rendered still more beautiful and striking. Indeed, all I can say to you at the end of these lectures (for we must come to an end at one time or other) is to express a wish that you may, in your generation, be fit to compare to a candle; that, in all your actions, you may justify the beauty of the taper by making your deeds honorable and effectual in the discharge of your duty to your fellow-men.

EXPERIMENTS

A word about
these experiments . . .

The experiments included in this section of the book are designed to help visualize or clarify some of the demonstrations made by Mr. Faraday in his lectures. They have been selected based on their relevance, safety and ease of preparation. All of them should be easily carried out in the simplest laboratory and many are suitable for duplication even in the home utility or workshop. Since most of them involve the use of fire and/or combustible materials, it is important that they are performed under suitable adult supervision and with necessary precautions for safety. A fire extinguisher should be readily available.

All of the twenty-two experiments in this section have been made by the publisher and are known to work as described. Before attempting an experiment, the description should be read carefully until the concept of the technique is understood. Most of these experiments have a generous margin for error, but, occasionally, an experiment may not work the first time it is tried. This is generally due to the necessity of making some slight adjustment to the procedure. If you should experience some difficulty in obtaining the desired results from an experiment, first reread the description to make certain all instructions have been

understood and followed. Then try the technique again, using common sense to make alterations to the procedure. The observations have been included in the descriptions so that experimenters can anticipate the results, and readers who are not doing the experiments can visualize the complete experiment.

Eric Schoch, of the Chemistry Department of Northwestern University's Technological Institute, has provided valuable assistance in the selection and content of these experiments.

Since it is not possible for us to control the circumstances under which these experiments are to be performed, we cannot assume any liability for injury to persons or property occurring as a result of any of these experiments.

Experiment 1

Objective

To isolate and collect the vapor produced by a burning candle and to demonstrate that it is this vapor which burns.

Technique and observations

❶ Hold a lighted match above the cold wick of a candle. Observe the wax in the wick melt and become fluid and finally take flame.

Blow out the candle quickly with a small, quick puff so as not to create turbulent air currents above the candle. You will notice a trail of vapor rising from the wick until the last spark of ember dies out in the wick. Again light the candle, but this time keep the lighted match ready as you extinguish the flame in the same manner. Draw the lighted match into the rising vapor trail. A small flame jumps quickly along the vapor trail to the wick and lights the candle. If you blow out the candle carefully you will find you can ignite the candle from a relatively great distance from the wick.

❷ Hold one end of a bent glass tube in the flame of the candle directly above the wick. You will know you have it in the correct position when a thick cloud of vapor travels through the tube and out the opposite end. You could experiment with lighting this vapor, as Faraday does in one of his demonstrations. You will probably need to draw out the end of the tube to a smaller diameter to create a smaller jet of vapor.

❸ While drawing out the vapor from a candle with a tube, collect the vapor in a large test tube or small flask. When the tube has become quite full of the vapor, remove the tube from the flame and test tube. If the test tube were stoppered and left to cool, the vapor would all condense back into a thin layer of wax on the walls of the test tube. As it is, some of the vapor will have already condensed onto the cool walls

Materials

— candle
— splints and/or matches
— glass tube (approx. ¼" diam.)
— test tube or small flask
— small bowl

of the test tube, but can be released again by gently warming the test tube over a flame.

❹ Pour the vapor quickly from the test tube into a shallow bowl which has been warmed slightly to discourage further condensation. If you immediately lower a lighted splint or match into the bowl, you will observe a slight explosion as all the vapor is ignited. You will also note that most of the vapor is consumed by that combustion.

Explanations

The candle is lit only when the wax in the wick has warmed enough to vaporize and ignite. Once the candle is lit, the heat of its own flame forms a small reservoir of liquid fuel around the base of the wick. This liquid is drawn up the candle wick where it becomes hot enough to vaporize. When the candle is blown out there is enough heat in the wick to continue the vaporization for a short time. The vapor is combustible, as is demonstrated by igniting the vapor trail from the candle and the collected vapor in the test tube. Finally, the wax coating in the test tube when the vapor is allowed to cool gives the clue to the origin and composition of this vapor.

Experiment 2

Objective
To examine the physical properties of a candle flame.

Technique and observations
❶ Construct a screen against which you may cast a shadow of the candle flame. This could be a white card which is viewed from the front or a translucent paper or plastic which may be viewed from behind. The advantage of using a translucent screen is that it will permit a closer inspection of the image without the problem of your own shadow interfering with your study.

❷ Set a burning candle flame in the path of a light beam projected at your screen. The beam could be direct sunlight if it is at a low enough angle or light from a projector or spotlight. The flame should be fairly close to the screen to create a sharp, clear image. Observe that the shadow of the flame is nearly a reverse image of the flame in that the brightest part of the flame casts the darkest shadow. If you have a good screen and an even spot of light you should also be able to see some of the air currents above and around the flame.

Explanations
The part of the flame which produces the most light casts the darkest shadow, indicating that it has the greatest density. The density is caused by particles of carbon in the vapor.

Materials
__ candle
__ projector, spotlight or direct sunlight
__ white card or translucent screen

Note—a translucent material such as tracing paper or waxed paper can be used for rear viewing or a regular sheet of typing paper can be prepared with a thin coating of a clear, light oil such as cooking oil.

Experiment 3

Materials

— light card or heavy
 paper
— candle

Objective

To demonstrate the area of greatest heat in the cross section of a candle flame.

Technique and observations

Take precautions for quick and safe disposal of a piece of burning paper in this experiment, as the paper is easily overheated, and often may catch fire.

❶ Lower a piece of heavy paper into the candle flame, being careful not to create a great turbulence around the flame. The card should be held just above the wick so that it is well below the tip of the normal flame, but not so low as to extinguish the flame. You will observe a scorched ring appear almost immediately on the top side of the card, and you should quickly remove the card from the flame to prevent its catching fire. [Note: the card should be *completely cold* to the touch before you discard it.]

Explanations

The scorching begins at the outer edges of the flame, indicating that the greatest heat is at the exterior surface of the flame where the availability of oxygen being drawn up the side of the candle supports the combustion. In other words, a fair description of the shape of the flame is that of a hollow, inverted cone.

Experiment 4

Objective

To demonstrate that something in the air is necessary for a candle to burn and that something in the air is consumed in the combustion of the candle.

Materials

__ candle
— jar
__ shallow pan

Technique and observations

❶ Place an overturned jar over a burning candle and observe the flame weaken and then die.

❷ Try the same experiment, only first mount the candle in the middle of a pan which is then partially filled with water. Place the overturned jar over the candle so that its rim is resting on the bottom of the pan and well below the surface of the water. The flame will go out, as before, but, in addition, some of the water will be drawn up into the jar. Mark the level of the water on the outside of the jar so you can determine approximately the proportion of the total volume of the jar which was taken up by water.

Explanations

The flame is extinguished because it has used up something in the air within the jar which supports combustion. Even though the vapor from the candle is combustible, combustion will not take place without a constant supply of good air. In the second part of the experiment, we find that water replaced part of the air in the jar, indicating that not all the air, but something in the air was consumed before combustion stopped.

The volume of air replaced by the water was approximately 1/5 of the total volume of air in the jar, which is about the same proportion as that of oxygen in the air. We can assume, then, that it is oxygen which is needed for and consumed during combustion.

Experiment 5

Materials

___ candle
___ window screen
 wire mesh

Objective

To cause incomplete combustion of a candle so as to be able to examine the vapor which is not burned. Also, to examine the procedure of quenching a flame by using a fine wire screen.

Technique and observations

❶ Place a lighted candle in an atmosphere where it burns well and is not disturbed by drafts.

❷ Using a small piece of metal window screening or other fine wire mesh, slowly lower screen into flame of candle. Observe the nature of the smoke or soot which you are causing to rise out of the flame. Compare this with the vapor you get by lowering the screen even further into the flame. When the screen dissects only the upper, brighter part of the flame the smoke is black and sooty. The smoke arising as the screen is lowered into the darker part of the flame is a gray vapor, similar to the vapor which proceeds from the wick shortly after a candle has been extinguished. You will also observe the bright ring at the level of the screen when it intersects the upper part of the flame. This demonstrates where the action of the flame is, as shown in Faraday's previous demonstration of a burned ring on a piece of paper held in the flame.

❸ While holding this screen in the lower part of the flame, add a second screen about ½″ above the first. By carefully adjusting the relative heights of these two screens, it is possible to ignite the vapor which comes up through the screens by holding a match close above the upper screen.

Explanations

The undisturbed candle burns brightly and cleanly with little smoke given off. The incomplete combustion caused by the screen in the flame give rise to a large amount of soot or

carbon particles. These carbon particles are the solid substances which are heated (and consumed) in the flame and give off light.

When you put the screen lower into the flame it gives off the unburned vapor which is produced from the heated liquid in the wick. Placing the second screen a small distance above the first allows air to mix with this vapor in sufficient quantity to support combustion again. But note that even though there was a combustible gas-like vapor above the screen, the heat of the flame was not sufficient above the screen to ignite it. This effect is what prompted Sir Humphrey Davy's invention of the miner's safety lamp. A screened enclosure for the flame prevented the ignition by that flame of any combustible gases in the area around the lamp. Gases entering the flame chamber through the screen would ignite but would not be in a quantity sufficient to explode. These gases would, however, burn with a colored haze which would indicate to the miner the presence of dangerous gases.

Experiment 6

Materials

__ torch
__ lime
(calcium hydroxide)

Objective
To demonstrate that solid substances in a flame give off light. To create limelight.

Technique and observations
For this experiment a very hot flame is required, preferably one that produces very little light. Faraday used a flame produced by hydrogen and oxygen burning together. A similarly hot flame can be had from an oxygen/propane torch available from many hardware stores and used in home workshops.

❶ Take a small lump of lime (calcium hydroxide) in a spoon. Insulate your hand from the handle of the spoon which is likely to get quite hot. Play the flame from the torch against the lump of lime. A bright white incandescence will proceed from the lime where it is hottest. A small piece of lime so heated will light up a darkened room as well as would a medium wattage light bulb. A stick of white chalk will also light up in the same manner.

Explanation
Flame tests of certain metals produce characteristic colors to the flame. Sodium is yellow, potassium is red and calcium orange red. Calcium hydroxide, when heated over a bunsen burner, will glow orange-red indicating the calcium. But because it has a melting point much higher than that of calcium alone, the hydroxide can be heated to extreme temperatures, producing limelight. This light was invented in 1816 by Thomas Drummond and used for theater spotlights in the mid-nineteenth century because of its superior brightness and the ease with which the small source could be focused using mirrors and lenses.

As Faraday points out, solid substances in a flame give off light. Pure calcium, heated to the same temperature, would

have melted *and* boiled away and would no longer give off light. The hydroxide, on the other hand, glows brightly under such a flame because it remains solid.

Experiment 7

Materials

__ burner
__ zinc strip
__ forceps or tweezers
__ clay crucible

Objective

To demonstrate the oxidation of zinc and to create Faraday's *philosophic wool.*

Technique and observations

❶ Hold the end of a strip of zinc in the flame of a burner. The zinc melts readily and will begin to sag at the end. Pull the strip from the flame and disengage the drop of molten zinc from the end. The end of the strip is now thin from being pulled by the weight of the drop.

❷ This thin metal, inserted into the flame of the burner, ignites with a brilliant bluish-green flame and leaves a strip of white substance. This substance glows yellow in the heat of the flame but cools to a clean white.

❸ Prepare some zinc filings by working the edge of a zinc strip with a metal file. Heat a clay crucible over a bunsen burner until it glows red. Sprinkle the filings into the hot crucible where they will ignite with a brilliant flame as did the sliver of zinc before. However, now you will see a cloud of white vapor proceed from the flame. This vapor cools and condenses readily into a light woolly mass.

Explanation

The low melting point of zinc, 419°C (790°F), makes it easy to melt a drop off of a zinc strip. It was necessary to make the strip thin at the end so it would not so readily conduct the heat away from the end in the flame and would, then, ignite. The ignited zinc burns in oxygen and the heat of the reaction results in a combination of zinc and oxygen atoms to form zinc oxide. The filings heat more rapidly and completely vaporize and ignite resulting in an oxide which cools to what appears to be a solidified vapor (flowers of zinc, or *philosopher's wool*). The ease with which zinc is vaporized and recondensed as an oxide makes it possible to purify it by

distillation. The resulting flowers of zinc can then be heated with carbon to process metallic zinc. The carbon reduces the zinc oxide by combining with the oxygen to be given off as carbon dioxide, leaving a bluish-white metal, zinc.

Zinc oxide is used as a permanent white pigment in paints, ceramics and cosmetics, and is also used in pharmaceuticals. It occurs in nature as the mineral zincite.

Experiment 8

— bunsen burner
— cotton ball
 or piece of yarn
— glass funnel
— turpentine

Objective

To release a stream of carbon particles from a flame and to super-heat them in a second flame.

Technique and observations

❶ Pour some turpentine into the metal cap from its container and set in the center of a metal pan (as a safety precaution.) Ignite a wick (cotton ball or strip of yarn) set in the turpentine cap. Dark smoke is given off and can be collected in an overturned jar held above the flame.

❷ An inverted funnel, held over the flame at an angle can be used to divert the smoke into the flame of a bunsen burner. The flame of the burner, normally a light blue, burns with a bright yellow light and consumes the smoke.

Explanation

The turpentine burns incompletely, giving off a cloud of unconsumed particles. These particles give off light when reheated and are then completely consumed in the combustion.

A smoking chimney is an indication of an inefficient fireplace or burner. The best designs provide a chamber which is heated by the fire through which the gases and smoke must pass before going up the chimney. In this super-heated atmosphere, with a sufficient supply of oxygen, they are reignited and consumed. This provides both more heat from the given fuel and less pollution of the interior of the chimney and the atmosphere.

Experiment 9

Objective
To demonstrate that water is a by-product of combustion.

Technique and observations

❶ Set up a glass laboratory funnel such that water condensing on the outside of the funnel can run down its spout and collect in a test tube.

❷ To keep the funnel cool, fold a piece of aluminum foil as you would a piece of filter paper for use in a funnel—in half and then in half again at right angles. This provides a pocket in the funnel to hold several ice cubes.

❸ Place a candle under the bowl of the funnel. Notice the drops of moisture that form on the outside of the funnel and eventually run down the stem into the test tube. If there is enough humidity in the air to create condensation on the glass without the candle, you will want to set up a second funnel as a control. This should be an identical funnel with about the same amount of ice in it, but without a candle. This way you can compare amounts of moisture collected from the two funnels.

If you can't produce two identical set-ups you can create a control comparison through time and measurement. First record the amount of time required to produce a measureable amount of water using a candle. Then collect the condensation from the air alone, without the candle for the same amount of time. The water collected from the combustion of the candle will be greater and if collected carefully will be close to the volume of candle burned.

Explanations
Water in the form of steam is produced during the combustion of a candle. The two properties of water—hydrogen and oxygen—are available respectively from the hydrocarbons of the candle and from the surrounding air. In

Materials
— candle
— glass funnel
— test tube
— aluminum foil
— ice

Experiment 4 we demonstrated that oxygen is consumed during combustion, and we now find that it has combined with the hydrogen in the process to form water.

Warm air has a greater capacity to hold water than cold air does, so that if the air is humid, or loaded with moisture, it too will give off some of its moisture in the form of condensation when it is cooled at the surface of the cold funnel. Therefore, it is necessary to compare the relative quantities of water collected for a more accurate picture of the amount of water given off in combustion.

Experiment 10

Objective
To demonstrate the expansion of water upon freezing.

Materials
__ plastic pill vial

Technique and observations

❶ Fill to the brim with water a plastic pill vial with a tight sealing plastic cap. (The "child-proof" caps are best.) Place the vial in the freezing compartment of a refrigerator or freeze by immersing it in a bowl of crushed ice and salt.

❷ When the water freezes it will expand beyond the capacity of the vial and either cause it to bulge or to crack open.

Note: Faraday's demonstration using iron bottles was probably more dramatic than the plastic pill vial, but in no case should anything be used that might cause injury upon breaking. The power of expansion of freezing water is considerable and is commonly the culprit in cold weather when bottles and water pipes burst as the water inside them freezes with no room for expansion.

Explanations
When water goes below 0° C (a fixed point of thermometers based on the freezing temperature of water) it solidifies in the form of crystals. The construction of these crystals is such that water takes up a greater amount of volume when frozen than when liquid. Because water expands upon freezing, a given volume of water contains more hydrogen/oxygen molecules than the same volume of ice. In other words, the density of ice is less than that of water which accounts for the fact that ice cubes float in a glass of water.

Experiment 11

Materials

__ metal container
__ burner

Objective

To demonstrate the expansion of water upon turning to steam.

Technique and observations

❶ For this experiment you will want a metal container with a tight fitting screw cap. A pint or quart size solvent can will work nicely. Put only enough water in the can to bring the level to about ½" depth. Leaving the cap off, bring the water to a rapid boil over a stove or bunsen burner.

Caution: if the container used has held thinner or other combustible liquid take the precaution of cleaning it thoroughly before using. An ammonia solution agitated in the container followed by several detergent rinses should be adequate. Rinse with clean water and dry before using over heat.

❷ When there is plenty of steam coming out of the opening, quickly remove the container from the flame and close the lid tightly (wear protective gloves as it will get hot quickly). You can now watch the container slowly collapse as it cools. If you place the container in a sink and pour cold water over it the effect will be even more dramatic.

Explanations

Water, brought to 100° C (a fixed point on thermometers based on the boiling point of water), boils and becomes a gas in the form of steam. The expansion of water as it becomes steam is great, so that just the little water which boiled off from the can displaced all of the air in the can and then some. When the container is sealed and cooled, the water vapor condenses back to a liquid state in which it takes up much less volume. Since air is prevented from re-entering the container, a vacuum has been produced, subjecting the can to atmospheric pressure on the outside which crushes the can inwards.

Note—Failure of the container to collapse could be caused by a poor seal at the cap or a broken seam. If the air leak is very small the fast cooling method should still result in a collapsed container.

Experiment 12

Objective
To construct a gas generator and use it for the preparation of hydrogen.

Technique and observations
Although the hydrogen generator which Faraday used in his lecture is most simple to construct, a safer and more controllable generator can be set up with little more effort.

❶ Two bottles are each prepared in the same way—with a two-hole stopper and two bent glass tubes. One glass tube extends nearly to the bottom of the bottle while the other is cut off just below the stopper. The two bottles are connected to each other by a small rubber tube between the two long glass tubes and fitted with a pinch-cock.

❷ Fill the first bottle halfway with diluted sulphuric or hydrochloric acid (about 1 part acid to 1 part water). The free end of glass tubing from that stopper should have a short piece of rubber attached to it. The other bottle should have a longer rubber tubing attached to its free end. It should be prepared with a layer of pebbles in the bottom on which the zinc strips are laid. The pebbles must hold the zinc strips above the opening of the long glass tube in that bottle.

To start a chemical reaction which will produce a gas, temporarily loosen the pinch-cock and blow into the short hose to force the acid into the second bottle. [**Caution:** do not inhale through this tube.] The acid rises above the zinc strips which begin to generate a gas. [**Caution:** Hydrogen and air can be explosive in containment, so do not have the apparatus near flames or direct heat until you can feel certain that the hydrogen has pushed the air from the bottle].

❸ Test for hydrogen issuing from the long hose by directing the escaping gas into an inverted test tube for a short while. Hydrogen, which is lighter than air, will go up into the test tube, eventually filling it. Remove the test tube from the

Materials
__ 2 bottles
__ 2 2-hole stoppers
__ glass tubing
__ rubber tubing
__ pinch-cock
__ pebbles
__ sulphuric acid
 (or hydrochloric acid)
__ zinc strips

❶

❷

❸

generator, holding it upside down, and pass a lighted match under its mouth. Hydrogen will burn with a sharp pop.

 Hydrogen may be collected under water by leading the tube into a trough. The gas bubbles up through the water and can be collected in bottles which have been filled with water and inverted into the trough. The gas displaces the water in the bottles as it bubbles into them. When you see that all the water is out of the bottles you then know you have a full container of hydrogen.

Note: the gas generator can be halted at any time simply by moving the pinch-cock from the connecting tube to the exit tube. The pressure of the gas which cannot now escape forces the acid back into the first bottle away from the zinc strips.

Explanations

Metals such as zinc and iron react with certain dilute acids to form a chemical compound and to liberate hydrogen from the acid. Not all metals and acids can be used to generate hydrogen: gold and silver are not active enough to replace the hydrogen in acids; and some acids (even concentrated sulphuric acid) are such strong oxidizers that they immediately oxidize the hydrogen to water.

Hydrogen is lighter than both air and water and although it can be collected by displacement in either environment, when collected under water it is easier to know when displacement is complete.

Experiment 13

Objective
To construct a small voltaic pile which generates a chemically induced electric current.

Technique and observations
Cut 10 to 20 disks each from copper sheet, zinc sheet, and felt. These disks should be about the size of a quarter. Soak the felt disks in a copper sulphate solution and drain off excess solution on a paper towel. Solder a short length of wire to a copper disk and a second wire to a zinc disk.

❶ Create a stack of the disks starting with the copper disk with the wire lead. Alternate disks in repeating order: copper, felt, zinc, copper, felt, zinc, etc. Top the pile with the zinc disc with the wire lead. Wrap the entire stack with rubber bands to hold it tightly together.

Contact the leads with a voltage meter. The strength of reading will depend on the size of the disks and the height of the pile.

Explanations
In the year 1800, Alessandro Volta created the first battery by this method, using a series of disks of silver, zinc, and cardboard soaked in salt water. In the voltaic cell we have constructed, chemical reactions take place between the metals and the copper sulphate solution. The metals are slowly being oxidized and the reaction separates negatively and positively charged ions, in the electrolyte, which each collect at the opposite poles. The negative ions collect at the copper disks (anode) and the positive ions at the zinc disks (cathode) opposite the copper sulphate disk. This causes a potential difference (voltage) between the two disks. Stacking the sandwiches increases the voltage just as when dry cell batteries are joined end to end.

Materials
— zinc sheet
— copper sheet
— felt strips
— copper sulphate
— bell wire
— rubber bands
— voltage meter

If you do not have access to soldering equipment it is possible simply to hold the wire leads against the end disks of the constructed pile.

❶

Experiment 14

Materials

__ mimeograph stencil
 (or parafine)
__ copper sheet
__ copper sulphate
__ burner
__ test tube
__ 6-volt battery
__ 2 wire leads

Objective

To electroplate with copper, using a copper solution and electricity. To use this process to etch a label onto a steel tool.

Technique and observations

Prepare a saturated copper sulphate solution by slowly adding copper sulphate crystals to a test tube about ⅓ full of boiling water. Stop adding the chemical when your solution is a rich blue color.

When the solution has cooled it will probably contain some crystals of copper sulphate which have reformed around the sides or on the bottom of the tube, indicating that the solution was super-saturated.

❶ Use either of two methods to prepare a stencil or design to be etched on the tool. (a) Type a clean stencil (with typewriter ribbon disengaged) of your name or initials onto a stencil sheet used for mimeograph machines. Cut out the stencil, leaving an inch or more around the typed area. Or (b) Work your stencil directly onto a clean tool, such as a knife-blade, by dipping it in melted parafine and scraping a design through the wax coating with a sharp tool. Parafine is hazardous if melted over direct heat. The container of parafine should be placed in a pot of boiling water until the wax becomes liquid.

❷ Set up the electroplating apparatus by attaching the positive lead from a 6 volt lantern battery to a copper sheet slightly smaller than the stencil. On top of the copper place a small piece of blotting paper or filter paper which has been soaked with the copper sulphate solution. Place the stencil over this (wrong-reading side UP) and place the tool to be labeled into contact with the stencil. The tool should be clean and free of oil or stains.

In the case of a parafine-coated object, the scraped design

is set in contact directly with the blotting paper. In either case, make certain that no unprotected metal part of your tool is in contact with the copper sulphate solution. Simply complete the circuit by contacting the tool with a lead from the negative pole of the battery. A sizzling sound may be heard and in a minute or two the battery leads can be disconnected revealing a copper design etched into the tool steel.

Explanation
The results of this experiment are typical of most ordinary electroplating processes. Certain substances (including salts such as copper sulphate), when dissolved in water, conduct electricity and are decomposed by it. These substances, called *electrolytes*, break down into positively and negatively charged atoms or *ions*, which are attracted to the opposite electrical poles. In this case the copper sulphate dissociates into positively-charged copper ions which are attracted to the cathode (negative pole) and sulphate ions which are attracted to the anode (positive pole). The current deposits a given amount of metal at the cathode, in this case the tool; and the anode, a sheet of copper, dissolves to the same extent. The copper sulphate solution is maintained relatively uniform.

Experiment 15

Materials

__ insulated wire
__ carbon rods (see note)
__ salt
__ 6-volt battery
__ beaker and test tubes

Objective

To demonstrate the decomposition of water using electricity. To produce oxygen and hydrogen for experimental use.

Technique and observations

❶ Strip the ends of two insulated wire leads and wrap the bare wire tightly around the ends of two carbon rods. Wrap the exposed wire with electrical tape so only the carbon rods are exposed at the ends of the leads.

Note: A source for carbon rods useful for this experiment can be obtained by cutting open a used D cell battery. The zinc casing can be cleaned and the black powder, manganese dioxide, can be spread out to dry and bottled. Both of these are useful in various experiments in this book.

The two wires are hooked up to a 6-volt battery (or a series of cells to create a similar voltage) and the carbon-tipped electrodes are lowered into a beaker of water. A very small amount of salt or sulphuric acid should be added to the water to make it electrically conductive.

❷ As current passes through the water, bubbles form and rise from each electrode. These bubbles can be collected by inverting water-filled test tubes over the carbon rods. Keep in mind that the bubbles will displace the water from the test tubes into the beaker which must be large enough to hold this extra water as well. The bubbles at the negative pole of the battery will be seen to form at twice the rate as at the positive pole. And the volume of water displaced from that tube will also be twice as great. When all water has been displaced from both tubes, disconnect the battery leads and tightly stopper the test tubes before pulling them out of the water.

Explanations

When a direct electric current is passed through water it is

decomposed into its two elements, hydrogen and oxygen because of ionic attraction to the electrodes.

The ions move toward the electrodes of opposite charge so that, in this case, the oxygen collects over the positive electrode (anode) and the hydrogen collects over the negative electrode (cathode). The two elements are each liberated from the compound as a gas. Hydrogen is collected at nearly twice the rate of oxygen, demonstrating the volumetric proportion of hydrogen to oxygen in water.

Experiment 16

Materials

— 3% hydrogen peroxide
— manganese dioxide
— 2 bottles
— 1 hole stopper
— glass tube
— rubber tubing

Objective

To generate oxygen chemically.

Technique and observations

❶ Fill a small bottle or jar about ⅓ full of 3% hydrogen peroxide. Test the air in the bottle by extinguishing a lighted splint and lowering the glowing ember into the bottle. The ember continues to die out. Now add a pinch or two of manganese dioxide to the solution and notice the boiling that takes place. Repeat the test of the air in the bottle. The glowing ember will now glow brightly and will possibly re-ignite.

❷ The oxygen may be collected by displacement of water, as was done for collecting hydrogen in Experiment 12. Stopper the bottle with a one-hole stopper fitted with a glass tube. From the glass tube extend a rubber tube into a trough of water and allow the bubbles to rise into the mouth of an upturned test tube or bottle, previously filled with water. The water will be displaced by the bubbles of oxygen which can then be saved for use in simple experiments requiring oxygen.

Explanations

Hydrogen and oxygen can combine to form two different compounds: water or hydrogen peroxide. Hydrogen peroxide has twice as much oxygen as water has, and it decomposes readily into water and oxygen.

In Faraday's method of preparing oxygen by heating potassium chlorate and manganese dioxide together, the manganese dioxide does not enter into the reaction. It acts as a *catalyst* in that it simply helps the oxygen to be liberated from the potassium chlorate without any change in itself. Similarly, with the hydrogen peroxide, the manganese dioxide causes a reaction which liberates oxygen more rapidly than would happen normally.

Experiment 17

Objective
To demonstrate the pressure of the air and how it changes. To construct a simple barometer.

Materials
__ beaker
__ flask
 (narrow-necked)
and/or
__ small bowl
__ balloon
__ drinking straw

Technique and observations
❶ Place a strip of tape on the neck of a narrow-necked flask. Make a series of evenly-spaced marks on the tape with a ballpoint pen. Then partially fill a beaker with warm water, insert the inverted flask, and allow to cool to room temperature.

When it reaches room temperature notice the level of water in the neck of the upturned flask. It will be higher than when you first inserted the flask. Check the level several times a day and notice any fluctuations in the water level. The fluctuations are likely to correspond to changes in the weather caused by high or low barometric pressure.

❷ Another sort of barometer can be constructed by stretching thin balloon rubber over a small bowl. A plastic drinking straw is attached by a drop of glue to the center of the rubber and a scale set up near the other end of the straw, which protrudes over the edge of the bowl. The position of the straw will correspond to the atmospheric pressure.

Explanations
These two simple barometers can be used to note changes in atmospheric pressure. When the pressure is high (usually associated with fine weather) the force exerted on the surface of the water in the beaker or on the rubber membrane increases, and both the column of water and the drinking straw indicator will rise.

Moist air weighs less than dry air, so the atmospheric pressure and our barometers drop when rain is imminent. The changes occur because we have isolated a volume of air from the atmosphere around it. As the atmospheric pressure

changes, a difference in pressure arises and the separating membrane (water in one case and rubber in the other) change positions, causing a change at our indicators.

Experiment 18

Objective
To illustrate the considerable force exerted by the pressure of air in our atmosphere.

Materials
__ drinking glass
__ bottle
__ card
__ handkerchief
__ acetate sheet

Technique and observations
Note: Perform these experiments in a place where a few spills will be of no consequence.

❶ Fill a drinking glass to the brim with water. Cover the glass with a piece of card and, while holding the card in place with one hand, invert the glass with the other. When you take your hand away from the card it remains there, and the water stays in the glass.

An even more remarkable demonstration can be made by covering the glass with a handkerchief. Hold the edges of the handkerchief around the glass while quickly inverting it. The water will remain in the glass despite the porousness of the cloth covering it.

If the glass is only about ½ full of water it will form a concave shape if you depress the handkerchief into the glass before turning it over. Stretching it tight forces air through the mesh; this air will then bubble up through the water giving an appearance of "boiling."

❷ From a thin sheet of acetate (such as that used for page protectors for notebooks) cut a disk just large enough to cover the mouth of a small bottle. With a hole-punch make a hole about ¼" round in the center of this disk. Fill your bottle to the brim with water and slide the disk over the mouth of the bottle. Then, holding the acetate by the edges, invert the bottle. Carefully remove your fingers from the disk. The water will remain in the bottle in spite of the hole in the disk. It is even possible to introduce toothpicks into the bottle through the hole without the water coming out.

Explanations

In every case the water is prevented from leaving the container while inverted because there is no way for air to enter above the column of water. Gravity, acting on the water, creates a vacuum above the water. However, it is not suction from the vacuum but pressure from the air which causes the water to remain in the glass. That point is best demonstrated by pushing the handkerchief into the partially filled glass. The air pressure forces it to curve inward rather than to bulge out under the weight of the water.

The water cannot pass through the hole in the acetate nor the mesh in the handkerchief due to the surface tension of the water. Even the ¼″ hole is not sufficient to permit a drop to form below it.

Experiment 19

Objective
To prepare limewater as a test for carbon dioxide (carbonic acid gas).

Technique and observations
Add about 1 teaspoon of calcium hydroxide to a pint of water. Stir vigorously. This makes a saturated solution which should be allowed to stand until all of the excess lime sinks to the bottom. Carefully pour off the clear liquid through filter paper into a storage bottle. Keep tightly capped.

❶ Fill a small jar about ¼ full of the limewater (calcium hydroxide solution). Lower a burning candle into the jar and cover the mouth of the jar to extinguish the flame. Pull the candle out, cap the jar and shake the limewater up with the air. The limewater turns milky.

❷ Exhale through a straw or glass tube into a small amount of the limewater. It also turns milky.

Explanations
Not all of the calcium hydroxide will dissolve in the water, indicating that the water has dissolved all it can and that we have a saturated solution. When the excess lime has settled and any which remains in suspension is filtered out the result is *limewater*.

Carbon dioxide reacts with limewater by changing calcium hydroxide to calcium carbonate. The carbonate is nearly insoluble in water and precipitates out of solution, causing the water to appear milky. The milkiness, then, indicates the presence of carbon dioxide.

Carbon dioxide is a by-product of combustion, and the fact that the air we exhale contains carbon dioxide shows us that combustion is part of our respiratory process.

Materials
— calcium hydroxide
— filter paper
— jar
— candle
— straw or glass tube

❶

❷

Experiment 20

Materials

__ gas generator
(see Exp. 12)
__ hydrochloric acid
__ marble chips
(calcium carbonate)
__ limewater
(see Exp. 19)

Objective

To prepare carbonic acid gas for laboratory use.

Technique and observations

Use a gas generator as set up for the generation of hydrogen in Experiment 12.

Partially fill the first bottle with diluted hydrochloric acid. The second bottle should contain a layer of pebbles with a layer of marble chips (calcium carbonate) on top. Blowing into the free hose on the acid bottle will force the acid into the other bottle where it will react with the calcium carbonate chips. The gas generated through the other free end can be collected by running a hose into a container of water and catching the bubbles in a water-filled inverted container. It is important to close the mouth of the container before removing it from the water.

❶ You can also bubble some of the gas through limewater as a test for carbon dioxide. The limewater turns milky. If you allow the gas to bubble through the limewater for a while longer, the milkiness will disappear. Now try bubbling the gas through a fresh solution of limewater. It turns milky, but if left will clear also.

Explanation

Hydrochloric acid reacts with marble chips (calcium carbonate) to form a solution of calcium chloride and water plus carbon dioxide gas. The gas is heavier than the air which explains the necessity to close the collecting container before removing it from the water. (See Experiment 21).

The carbon dioxide bubbles through the limewater, creating an insoluble milky suspension of calcium carbonate particles. When the reaction between the calcium hydroxide and carbon dioxide is complete, the continued presence of carbon dioxide begins to convert the calcium carbonate to

calcium bicarbonate. The bicarbonate of calcium is soluble in water, so it returns into solution and the water becomes clear again.

Experiment 21

Materials

__ 2 candles
__ 2 beakers
__ baking soda
__ vinegar

Objective

To demonstrate that carbon dioxide is heavier than air.

Technique and observations

❶ Suspend two small, lighted candles inside a beaker or jar so that their respective flames are about one-third and two-thirds of the distance below the rim. In another beaker or jar, mix a couple of spoonfuls of baking soda with a capful of vinegar.

The baking soda will react with the vinegar. After the reaction has continued for some time, pour the air from that beaker slowly into the one with the candles. Pour the gas just as if it were water. First the lower candle will be extinguished and shortly after the upper one will go out.

Explanation

The baking soda (sodium bicarbonate) and the vinegar (acetic acid) react to release carbon dioxide as a gas. Being a heavier gas than air, the carbon dioxide stays in the beaker and can be poured from one container to another. The candles are used to help visualize the level of the gas as the second container is being filled.

Experiment 22

Objective
To show the effect of oxygen on combustion.

Technique and observations
Using the techniques described in Experiment 16, prepare a small jar of oxygen. An easily-removed stopper or a piece of glass to cover the jar between experiments will prevent premature escape of the oxygen.

❶ Cut a strip of tin about ¼″ wide and 4 to 6 inches long. Bend a small hook in the end to hold samples.

Place a sample of powdered charcoal in the bend of the tin strip and heat it over the flame of a burner. When the charcoal begins to glow red, uncover the mouth of the oxygen jar and lower the hot charcoal into it. [**Caution:** For safety, never use a large sample, and keep yourself clear from the area above the jar's opening, as burning particles sometimes shoot upwards from the sample]. The charcoal, which was only partly glowing when inserted, will be consumed in a brilliant spark of light.

Other samples you might try are sulphur and steel wool. Both of these should be heated over the burner first before inserting in the jar of oxygen. The sulphur burns with a light blue flame over the burner but becomes a brilliant, vigorous flame in the oxygen. The steel wool glows red over the burner, but will burst into flame in the oxygen.

Faraday used oxygen in which to burn turpentine. This can be easily accomplished. A small tuft of cotton can be pinched in the end of the tin strip and dipped into turpentine. Pass it through a flame to ignite the fuel. The flame burns brightly but with considerable smoke. In the oxygen jar the flame burns more brilliantly and the smoke stops.

Materials
__ oxygen
__ burner
__ strip of tin
__ powdered charcoal
__ sulphur
__ steel wool

❶

117

Explanation

The charcoal burning in the air creates a reaction between carbon and oxygen in which the carbon burns (or is oxidized) to form carbon dioxide. In oxygen, the combustion is complete and rapid because there is plenty of oxygen available.

Since *combustion* is *oxidation*, it takes place more rapidly in pure oxygen than in the mixture of oxygen and other gases in the atmosphere.

GLOSSARY

Argand lamp—a lamp with a tubular wick which admits a current of air inside as well as outside the flame.

bell jar—a type of glass vessel open at the bottom and closed at the top like a bell.

bladder—a flexible or stretchable membrane.

calcareous—consisting of, or containing, calcium carbonate or carbonate of lime; also, containing the element calcium.

camphene—rectified oil of turpentine, used for burning in lamps.

cane—any hollow or pithy jointed stem.

capillary attraction—the kind of action which makes two things which do not dissolve in each other still hold together.

carbonic acid—an acid, H_2CO_2, existing only in solution. It breaks up readily into water and carbon dioxide, CO_2, which was commonly called *carbonic acid* or *carbonic acid gas*.

chlorate of potassa—potassium chlorate.

coal-gas—gas made from coal; specifically that made by distilling bituminous coal in retorts; it was used for lighting and heating. It consists chiefly of hydrogen and methane, with small amounts of carbon monoxide, nitrogen, ethylene, etc.

collodion—a viscous liquid consisting of a mixture of alcohol and ether in which soluble gun-cotton or pyrozylin is dissolved. On evaporation of the solvents the pyrozylin remains in a tough adhesive form which was used as a coating for wounds, for photographic films, etc.

condensation—the process of reducing a substance to another, denser form. For example, steam to water or air to the condition of a liquid. This is generally done by a decrease in temperature or an increase in pressure.

Davy lamp—a miner's lamp constructed with a view to avoiding explosions in an atmosphere containing inflammable gas. In the most common form, of which the original Davy lamp, invented by Sir Humphrey Davy, is an example, the flame is enclosed by fine wire gauze which, owing to its cooling effect, prevents the flame from passing.

dips—candles made of lengths of cotton cut off, hung up by a loop, dipped in melted tallow, taken out again and cooled, then redipped until there is an accumulation of tallow round the cotton.

electrolysis—the process of chemical decomposition by the action of an electric current.

electroplating—a process for covering an object with an adhering coating of metal, by means of electrolysis.

elements—chemical substances out of which we can not get anything else; elementary substances.

gas—*cf.* vapor—according to Faraday, a gas differs from a vapor in that a gas remains permanent whereas a vapor will condense.

Leyden jar—a device for storing charges of static electricity; commonly made with layers of foil lining the inner and outer surfaces of a jar or bottle. A brass knob projects on a spike through the stopper of the bottle, and is connected to the inner layer of foil. The charge is released when contact is made between the knob and the outer layer of foil.

limelight—an intense light produced by the incandescence of a stick or ball of lime in the flame of a combination of oxygen and hydrogen gases or of oxygen and coal gas. Limelight was commonly used as theatrical lighting.

lycopodium—a fine, yellowish powder composed of the spores of the club moss (*Lycopodium clavatum*). The substance is highly inflammable and is used in the manufacture of fireworks and for the artificial representation of lightning.

marble—a stone which is a compound of carbonic acid and lime.

muriatic acid—hydrochloric acid. (The acid was originally believed to be an oxide of a nonexistent element, murium; at that time, *muriatic acid* was its accepted scientific name.

natural philosopher—as defined by Faraday, a "natural philosoher" was one who was "constantly employed in observing the works of nature, and tracing the manner in which she directs the order and arrangement of the world. He always preferred the term natural philosopher to that of physicist or chemist.

paraffine—a fatty material obtained from petroleum.

paraffine oil—kerosene.

oil of vitriol—sulphuric acid

powdered lead—in his experiments with powdered lead, Faraday used lead pyrophorus which he obtained by heating dry tartrate of lead in a glass tube closed at one end and drawn to a fine point at the other, until no more vapors were evolved. The open end he then sealed. When the tube is broken, and the contents shaken into the air, they burn with a red flash.

salt—any of a class of compounds formed when a hydrogen atom of an acid is partly replaced or wholly replaced by a metal, or metal-like radical.

snapdragon—a game, generally played at Christmas in Great Britain, in which raisins are snatched from a vessel containing burning brandy.

sperm oil—the purified oil of the spermaceti whale.

spirit—alcohol

stearin—any fat was considered to be made of olein, which consisted of the liquid or oily part, and stearin, which consisted of the solid part.

The more precise chemical definition in use presently is that stearin is an ester of glycerol and stearic acid.

sucker—a toy consisting of a round piece of leather with a string through the center, which, when wetted and laid upon a smooth surface and drawn up by the string, adheres due to the vacuum created. A game was played with this toy in which the winner is the one to lift the largest stone with the sucker.

sulphuric acid—sulphur trioxide.

tallow—harder kinds of fat, procured from oxen or sheep, used for candle- and soap-making.

vapor—the gaseous state of a substance, especially one that is liquid or solid at room temperature.

Voltaic pile—originally a vertical series of alternate discs of two dissimilar metals such as copper and zinc, arranged with disks of cloth or paper moistened with acid layered between them; used for producing a current of electricity; a battery.

watch-glass—a glass for covering the face of a watch; a watch crystal.

whitening—a composition of lime and water used for whitening walls, whitewash.

wire gauze—wire screen similar to a window screen, sieve or strainer.

INDEX

124

10/94 2
27 2/00
29 11/06